The Life and Times of
François-Charles Nagot, P.S.S.,

Founding Superior of the Sulpicians in the U.S.

Thomas R. Ulshafer, P.S.S.

Cover painting by Peter Wm. Gray. P.S.S.

Layout and cover design by William (Billy) Mitchell.

Printed by J. H. Furst Printing Co., Inc.

Table of Contents

Acknowledgements iv
Abbreviations v
Preface vi

Part One: France

I. Birth and Childhood 1
II. Education and Formation 11
    Primary Education 11
    College of Tours 11
    The Seminary of Saint Sulpice in Paris 15
III. First Sulpician Assignment: Nantes (1760-1768) 25
IV. Leadership of the *Robertins* (1769-1781) 35
V. Leadership of the *Petit Séminaire* (1781-1789) 41
VI. Ministry at the *Grand Séminaire* (1789-1791) 55
VII. Visit to England 57
VIII. Voyage to the United States 67

Part Two: The United States

IX. The New World 81
X. A Promising Start 89
XI. Years of Disappointment and Conflict (1791-1801) 93
    Low Enrollment 94
    Conflict with Former Jesuits 96
    Financial Difficulties 102
    The Founding of St. Mary's College 107
    Emery and Developments in France 110
    Health Problems 116
    Other Experiences 120
XII. Turning Some Corners (1802-1810) 129
    The Seminary 129
    The College 130
    Pidgeon Hill and Emmitsburg 132
    Emery's Last Years 140
    Publications 144
    Other Experiences 147
    Failing Health and Resignation 153
XIII. Final Years (1811-1816) 157
Conclusion 165

Bibliography 167

Acknowledgements

The German theologian Dietrich Bonhoeffer once wrote, "It is so easy to overestimate the importance of our own achievements compared with what we owe to the help of others." Sharing this sentiment, I acknowledge that this project would not have been possible without the contributions of many people. To begin with, I am very grateful to my superiors in the Society of Saint Sulpice for supporting me throughout this project. First, the provincial council of the U.S. Province of the Sulpicians kindly gave me the opportunity to do this project by granting me a sabbatical for the academic year 2015-2016. Second, our Superior General Father Ronald D. Witherup, P.S.S., accompanied me on my travels in France, assisted me with locating some missing materials in Paris, and gave me very helpful recommendations on the text itself. Third, my Provincial Father John C. Kemper, P.S.S., encouraged me and collaborated with Father Thomas R. Hurst, P.S.S., president rector of St. Mary's Seminary & University, to see that my study was professionally printed and appropriately distributed.

I also received much professional help from historians, archivists and librarians. These included: Dr. Tricia Pyne and Ms. Alison Foley of the Associated Archives at St. Mary's Seminary & University in Baltimore; Father Jean Longère, P.S.S., and Ms. Agnès Jaurégibéhère of the Sulpician Archives in Paris; Mr. Marc Lacasse of the Sulpician Archives in Montreal; Sr. Betty Ann McNeil, D.C., of DePaul University in Chicago; Mr. Thomas Raszewski and the staff of the Knott Library at St. Mary's Seminary & University; and Ms. Anne-Violaine Jarlégant of the Municipal Archives of Tours, France. Dr. Pyne also advised me on the text.

I would conclude by gratefully acknowledging the help I received from a few others. First, two translators helped me decipher some old handwritten French documents. They were Mr. Bruno Delorme of St. Mary's Seminary & University and Sr. Marie Lorraine Bruno, I.H.M., of Immaculata University in Scranton. Second, Father Richard M. Gula, P.S.S., reviewed the final draft of the study and gave me many helpful suggestions. Finally, I am grateful to the National Library of France and to Google Books for their on-line services. Without them, it would have been difficult, if not impossible, to access some publications from the 18th and 19th centuries.

— *Thomas R. Ulshafer, P.S.S*

Abbreviations

AA   Associated Archives at St. Mary's Seminary & University in Baltimore
ADIL   Departmental Archives of Indre-et-Loire in Tours
AMT   Municipal Archives of Tours, Historical Section
BnF   National Library of France (http://gallica.bnf.fr)
GB   Google Books (https://books.google.com)
MdHS   Maryland Historical Society
SAM   Sulpician Archives in Montreal
SAP   Archives of the Society of Saint Sulpice in Paris

FATHER OLIER
FOUNDER OF THE SOCIETY OF ST. SULPICE

Preface

This brief Preface is intended to give readers background that they may need to appreciate "The Life and Times of François-Charles Nagot, P.S.S." The initials after Father Nagot's name stand for "[Society of the] Priests of Saint Sulpice," and the needed background consists of some basic information about this community to which he belonged.

The 17th century was a period of serious reform and intense renewal for the Catholic Church in France. Mainly because of religious wars that took place there in the second half of the 16th century, many of the changes that had been mandated by the Council of Trent (1545-1563) only began to take place in France in the 17th. They were promoted by such people as Cardinal Pierre de Bérulle, Saint Vincent de Paul, and Saint John Eudes. Among this group was a young priest-aristocrat named Jean-Jacques Olier (1608-1657) who gave up the pursuit of a very promising ecclesiastical career to become the hands-on pastor of Saint-Sulpice near Paris, perhaps the largest and most challenging parish in France at the time.

Because Olier believed that the reform and renewal of the Church in France would not be successful unless the priesthood was reformed and renewed, he gathered together a group of like-minded diocesan priests and established a seminary at his parish. This group became known as the Society of the Priests of Saint Sulpice and it was dedicated to serving the renewal of the Church by promoting excellence in the formation of its diocesan priests. So successful was Olier's venture at Saint Sulpice in Paris that gradually bishops from all over France asked him to send teams of his priests to their dioceses to establish similar seminaries there. Eventually Olier's community received official recognition from the Holy See.

THE CHURCH OF SAINT-SULPICE
17TH CENTURY (BNF)

The ministry of Father François-Charles Nagot cannot be appreciated without realizing that he became a member of this community and so saw his specific vocation as a call to do priestly formation above all. At the same time, to make full sense of his emigrating to the U.S. late in his life, it is necessary to know that he, like the other followers of Olier, saw priestly formation in a larger context, as part of a larger movement of evangelization and renewal in the Church. In fact, during Olier's own lifetime, he had planned to send some of his priests as missionaries to France's colony in North America, now Quebec. Centered in Montreal, they would not only engage in priestly formation but would also evangelize the native peoples and minister to Catholic settlers in a vast region.

Because the Society of the Priests of Saint Sulpice has always been a small society and because its ministry takes place primarily in seminaries, it does not have high visibility to the Catholic laity. Yet, because of the success of the Sulpicians in their primary ministry and because of their historic commitment to evangelization, there are now Sulpicians on five continents. Father Nagot's transfer from France to the U.S. was one important step in this four-century process of evangelization and also marked the start of priestly formation in this country.

INTRODUCTION

During 2016 the Sulpician Fathers in the United States are celebrating the 225th Anniversary of the arrival of the first Sulpicians in this country. Coincidently, April 9, 2016 is also the 200th Anniversary of the death of Father François-Charles Nagot, P.S.S. (1734-1816), the leader of that first band of Sulpicians and the founder of St. Mary's Seminary and University in Baltimore, our nation's first Catholic seminary. Therefore, it seemed appropriate to prepare a biographical sketch of Father Nagot that would include all the information available.[1]

However, not long after this project began, it became clear that there is very limited information about Father Nagot and his activities, especially prior to 1781 when, at the age of 47, he was appointed superior of the *Petit Séminaire* in Paris. Father Nagot's reserved personality and legendary simplicity and humility undoubtedly contributed to this. However, the nature of his ministry was probably a more important factor. Sulpician historian Father Joseph Ruane once wrote, "Father Nagot's life is hardly the subject of history; it does not contain the grand deeds about which history is usually written; it was the simple, hidden life of a seminary director."[2]

Father Nagot lived in tumultuous times when the American and French Revolutions rocked Europe and America, with immense implications for the Catholic Church. Therefore, this anniversary study will both summarize the facts, limited at times, that we do know about Father Nagot's life, and present a

---

1 There is currently no biography of Father Nagot. The closest thing we have is his official obituary, first published in France at the time of his death. For that document, see [Antoine Garnier?], "*Necrologie*," in *L'ami de la religion et du roi*, VIII (Paris: Le Clere, 1816), 286-288. This document is focused primarily on his ministry in France. It was republished subsequently in Guy-Toussaint-Julien Carron, *Pensées ecclésiastiques pour tous les jours de l'année*, 5th ed., V (Paris: Rusand, 1823), 177-182. It was also translated into English and published in an abridged version in London. See *Catholicon: or, the Christian Philosopher*, III, July-Dec., 1816 (London: Keating, Brown and Keating, 1816), 80. There exists another 19th century document that was based on the French obituary but that added a few details. See [Étienne Michel Faillon?], "*Notice sur François Charles Nagot*" (Baltimore: handwritten document in the AA, n.d. [1861?]). Sulpician Father Louis Bertrand also wrote a brief biography of Nagot that is based heavily on the preceding documents. See his *Bibliothèque sulpicienne; ou, Histoire littéraire de la Compagnie de Saint-Sulpice*, II (Paris: Picard, 1900), 37-45. Some of what is known about Nagot's life in the U.S. is covered in the standard histories of the Society of Saint Sulpice and of St. Mary's Seminary & University in Baltimore. See Joseph William Ruane, *The Beginnings of the Society of Saint Sulpice in the United States (1791-1829)* (Baltimore: The Voice of the Students and Alumni of St. Mary's Seminary, 1935); Charles G. Herbermann, *The Sulpicians in the United States* (New York: The Encyclopedia Press, 1916); Christopher J. Kauffman, *Tradition and Transformation in Catholic Culture: The Priests of Saint Sulpice in the United States from 1791 to the Present*. (New York: Macmillan, 1988); and Étienne-Michel Faillon, *Histoire du séminaire de Saint-Sulpice de Baltimore et les divers établissements aux quels il a donné naissance*, 2 vols. (Baltimore, MD: unpublished bound manuscript in the Collection of the Associated Sulpicians of the U.S. at the AA, 1861).

2 Ruane, 94. Ruane, however, failed to note that he was known outside the seminary among clerics in France and in Britain. As we have seen, obituaries of Nagot were published in both countries.

socio-historical context for his life both in France and in the United States. We will learn a lot about his times by learning about the experiences of some of his friends and acquaintances. This will enable us to understand him better. Hence the title, "The Life and Times of François-Charles Nagot, P.S.S."

Four themes will recur throughout this study. First, Father Nagot was an outstanding Sulpician priest who was widely considered a very holy and prayerful man. We will learn about his impact on the lives of some of those whom he touched. Second, Father Nagot was an experienced leader even before he came to the U.S. Many of his accomplishments here were consistent with and flowed from his earlier accomplishments in France.[3] Third, Father Nagot was focused on his specific ministry and on the needs of the Church.[4] Nevertheless, major international political events had a profound effect on him not only during his years in France but also while he was in the U.S. Fourth, the standard histories of the Society of Saint Sulpice and of St. Mary's Seminary & University do not, at times, give enough credit to Father Nagot for what was accomplished during his nineteen years as superior in the U.S. Rather, they tend to give more credit to his superiors and to his gifted collaborators who later rose above him in the Church.[5] Nevertheless, this study will show that the Sulpicians and St. Mary's Seminary and University would not be here today had it not been for his profound dedication to his Sulpician vocation and his strength of character.

---

3 Some historians seem to have known only a little about Nagot's life in France. See, for example, Herbermann, 54-55.

4 Nagot left us no writings on his political views. From what we do know about him, his thinking in this area may have been something like that of the traditional French *parti dévot* in that: he put the interests of the Church before those of the state, he was a moderate monarchist, and he was opposed to the influence of Protestantism and Jansenism in France. On the *parti dévot*, see, e.g., Dale K. Van Kley, *The Religious Origins of the French Revolution: from Calvin to the Civil Constitution, 1560-1791* (New Haven: Yale University, 1966).

5 Another factor here was Father Nagot's strong belief in Sulpician collegiality. When he spoke or wrote, he often did so in the name of the local Sulpician community, not merely in his own name. Moreover, he was not afraid to delegate responsibility to others with ability.

Part One
FRANCE

Birth and Childhood

The story of François-Charles Nagot began in 1734 in the small French city of Tours, located about 150 miles south-southwest of Paris. Tracing its origins to Roman times, Tours in the 18th century was the capital of the royal province of Touraine.[1] It was also a fairly prosperous commercial center due to two features of its geography. First, it was centrally located on the banks of the Loire River, an artery of trade that ran from the region around Lyons and Bourges in the east to the Atlantic Ocean, not far west of the port city of Nantes. Second, it sat astride a significant north-south road that connected Paris with Aquitaine and other points south.

Tours was more important as a religious center due to the fact that the remains of Saint Martin of Tours (c. 316 - c. 397), Apostle of the Gauls, were enshrined there. A converted Roman soldier, Saint Martin became Tours' third bishop. The huge gothic Basilica of Saint Martin which housed his remains became a principal destination for pilgrims in the middle ages. Sadly, in 1562 the Huguenots, or French Protestants, sacked the church and demolished Saint Martin's tomb.[2] When Nagot was born, nevertheless, the impressive but aged basilica was still a place where the Saint and his relics could be venerated.[3]

SAINT MARTIN OF TOURS WINDOW AT
OLD SAINT MARY'S CHAPEL IN BALTIMORE

---

1 Today it is the administrative center of the French Department of Indre-et-Loire.

2 The silver and gold art treasures that were melted down to finance the Protestant cause are described in Charles de Grandmaison, *Procès-verbal du pillage par les Huguenots des reliques et joyaux de Saint Martin de Tours* (Tours: Maine, 1863).

3 The medieval Basilica of St. Martin of Tours was nationalized during the French Revolution and later razed. The remains of the tomb of St. Martin were rediscovered in 1860, and that led to the construction of a new Basilica, completed in 1902.

It is also worth noting that Saint Martin and his shrine in Tours played an important role in the piety of Father Jean-Jacques Olier (1608-1657), founder of the Society of Saint Sulpice. Since the time of his conversion, Olier had greatly admired Saint Martin for his profound humility,[4] and occasionally Olier spent time at the Abbey of Marmoutiers that was founded by Saint Martin on the outskirts of Tours. As Nagot himself would write, in November 1653 Olier made a deeply moving visit to the Basilica of Saint Martin.[5] Shortly after that visit, he entered into a mutual agreement with the canons of that shrine – the Basilica was a collegial church – whereby they and his community in Paris would be united in a spiritual association of prayer and good works under Saint Martin's patronage.[6] Thus, Saint Martin became one of the principal patrons of the Society of Saint Sulpice.[7]

THE MEDIEVAL BASILICA OF SAINT MARTIN OF TOURS

---

4 Étienne-Michel Faillon, *Vie de M. Olier, fondateur du Séminaire de S. Sulpice,* 1st ed., I (Paris: Poussielgue-Rusand, 1841), 304.

5 François-Charles Nagot, *Vie de M. Olier, Curé de S. Sulpice* (Versailles: J. A. Lebel, 1818), 449-450.

6 Nagot described Olier's reason for this initiative as follows: "*La piété qu'il avoit remarquée dans cette illustre compagnie* [i.e., *le chapitre de cette insigne église*], *son attachement à la doctrine de l'Église et sa soumission au saint siège, dont elle a toujours fait la profession la plus ouverte comme la plus invariable, lui faisoient espérer, soit pour lui-même, soit pour sa communauté et son séminaire, s'il en obtenoit des lettres d'association, une protection spéciale du saint évêque de Tours, qu'elle invoque dans la basilique dédiée sous son nom.*" Ibid.

7 Ibid. 449. We have no evidence that Nagot knew of the Olier-connection in his early years. Later in his life, as we shall see, he had a friendship with one of the canons of the Basilica.

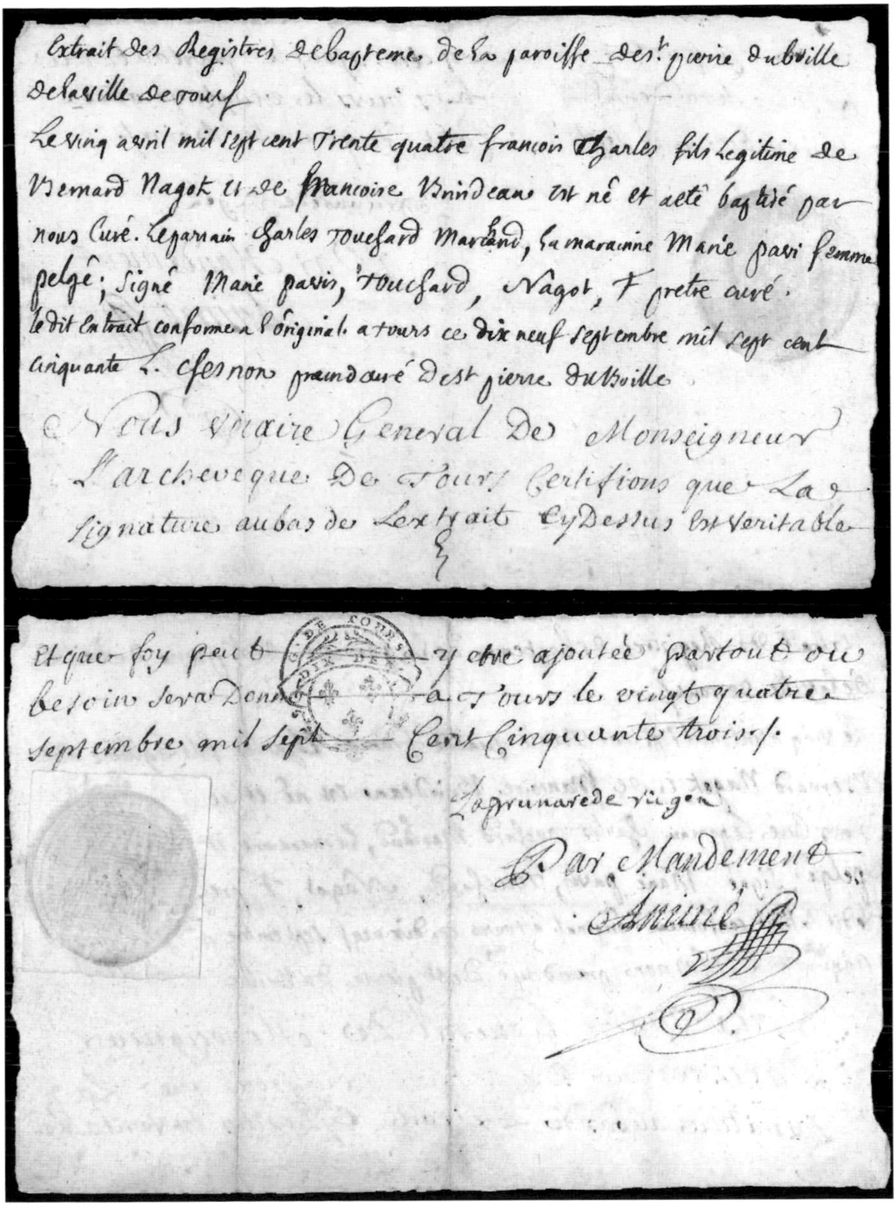

Extrait des Registres de baptême de la paroisse de St pierre dubroille
de la ville de tours

Le ving avril mil sept cent Trente quatre françois Charles fils Legitime de
Bernard Nagot et de françoise Bindeau est né et a été baptié par
nous Curé. Le parrain Charles Touchard Marchand, la maraine Marie pari femme
pelgé, Signé Marie paris, Touchard, Nagot, F pretre curé.
Le dit Extrait conforme a l'original. a tours ce dix neuf septembre mil sept cent
cinquante L. Chesnon grand curé dest pierre Dubroille

Nous Vicaire General De Monseigneur
L'archeveque De Tours Certifions que La
Signature au bas de L'extrait Cy Dessus Est Veritable

Et que foy peut   y être ajoutée partout ou
besoin sera Donné   a tours le vingt quatre
septembre mil sept   Cent Cinquante trois.

La grunarede vagon

Par Mandement

Amirié

NAGOT'S BAPTISMAL CERTIFICATE

7

It was in this historic city of Tours that, on April 20, 1734, François-Charles Nagot was born.[8] Since there are several saints with the name Francis, we do not know for sure which one he was named after,[9] but we do know that his second given name came from Saint Charles Borromeo, the great founder of seminaries, since that saint's feast day was also celebrated as Nagot's personal feast day.[10]

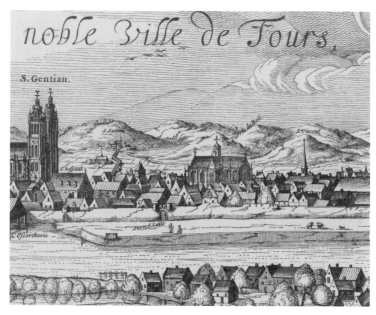

SAINT-PIERRE-DU-BOILLE (AMT)

8 There is some confusion about the precise date of Nagot's birth. Most official sources, including his published French obituary and the old official register of members of the Society of Saint Sulpice in Paris, say that he was born on April 19. However, his baptismal certificate says that he "was born and was baptized" ("*est né et été baptisé*") on April 20. Accordingly, the *fichiers généalogiques* at the AMT also list April 20, 1743 as his birthday. Finally, he himself stated that "*die vigesima Aprilis*," i.e., April 20, was his date of birth. See François Charles Nagot, Untitled Instructions for Epitaph (Baltimore: handwritten document in Nagot personal papers in the Collection of the Associated Sulpicians of the U.S. at the AA, Jan. 10, 1810). In another document in his hand, he wrote, "*J'ai été baptisé le 20 d'avril 1734 jour de ma naissance.*" See F. C. Nagot, "*Confitebor tibi in directione cordis*" (Baltimore: handwritten paper in Nagot personal papers in the Collection of the Associated Sulpicians of the U.S. at the AA, n.d.), 9. This study defers to his own statements about the date of his birth.

9 It may well have been the Frenchman St. Francis de Sales, an evangelizer who established an important early seminary in Geneva. Among Nagot's personal papers in the Collection of the Associated Sulpicians of the U.S. at the AA, there is a large holy card bearing the image of this St. Francis, canonized in 1665. St. Francis de Sales was also an important figure for Olier.

10 See Jean Tessier, *Epoques du Séminaire de Baltimore.* trans. J. Kortendick (Baltimore: handwritten manuscript in the AA, 1804), 18-19. Nagot signed virtually every letter only as "Nagot." There are a few instances where he also used his first two initials. However, in the *Ancien Regime*, many Frenchmen used their second given name as their common name of address, and since Saint Charles Borromeo was celebrated as Nagot's patron, his family and close friends almost certainly called him Charles.

On the same day, April 20, he was baptized by his pastor, designated only as "F priest pastor," at the Church of Saint-Pierre-du-Boille. This was Tours' oldest parish and it was located in the center of town, near the imposing Cathedral of Saint-Gatien (Lat. *Gatianus*).[11] The parish's Baptismal Register states that he was the son of Bernard [-Armand] Nagot, a merchant, and Françoise Brindeau.[12] His parents had been married eight years earlier at the neighboring Church of Saint Vincent, his mother's parish, and he was the sixth of their thirteen children, several of whom died before they reached the age of 21. His godfather was a merchant named Charles Touchard, and his godmother was a married woman named Marie Pavi Pelgé.[13] Beyond these essential facts and a few related details, we know nothing more about his early childhood.

---

11 The church building was nationalized during the French Revolution and was razed. See also Jean-Louis Chalmel, *Histoire de Touraine jusqu'à l'année 1790,* III (Paris: Fournier, 1828), 534-535.

12 This register is held in the AMT.

13 Much of this information is from the *fichiers généalogiques* in the AMT. His godmother's name, translated literally, reads "Marie Pavi [or Pavis] [married] woman [i.e., wife] Pelgé." Until the 20th century, this was a common way to give the name of a married woman in such records. There is a record of a 1726 marriage at St. Pierre du Boille of a Marie Pavie [or Pavy] to a man named René Joseph Pelgé de la Verrierie, who became a prominent commercial magistrate (*juge-consul*) in that city. It is likely that this Marie was the godmother of Nagot. See Patrice Morette-Bourny, "*fiche généalogiques*," at http://morette-bourny.org/fiches/fiche1206.htm#f1206 (accessed 2/13/16). In this context, it should be noted that the spelling of names in the 18th century was often inconsistent and based on how they sounded.

II.

EDUCATION AND FORMATION

Primary Education

For his primary education, like most other French children of that time who lived in urban areas, François-Charles Nagot would probably have attended a so-called *petite école* for boys, a kind of parochial school, in his native town.[1] There he would have been given both basic religious instruction and instruction in "the three R's."[2] This kind of schooling normally began at the age of 7 and it was under the direction of a schoolmaster (*maître d'école*) licensed by the local bishop. The schoolmaster was supervised by the local pastor who paid him. The pastor was also responsible for providing additional religious instruction to the young people of his parish, and Nagot may have learned elementary Latin either at his primary school or from a priest of his parish, as did his contemporary Jacques-André Emery (1732-1811). We do not know.

College of Tours

The young Nagot then progressed to the next level of education, namely the College of Tours that was under the direction of the Jesuits.[3] We have only a little information about this part of his education because, starting in 1762, the Jesuits were suppressed in France, and their records from schools like the one in Tours were largely lost.[4]

From other sources, however, we know that the college in Tours was one of about 90 similar Jesuit institutions in France in the mid-18th century.[5] From the beginning, the Jesuits preferred to admit "mature students who had already learned to read and write."[6] At that time, education in these schools was generally free of charge – the Jesuit colleges in France were endowed and

---

1 There were also primary schools run by religious congregations who specialized in providing education to children from very poor families. The system is described succinctly by H. C. Barnard, *Education and the French Revolution* (London: Cambridge U. Press, 1969), 1-16.

2 Alexandre Ott, *Sur l'instruction primaire: l'ancien régime, la révolution, l'époque actuelle* (Nancy: Imprimerie Nanciénne, 1880), 5-13. Ott tells us that the heads of primary schools were often ordinary laypersons. See also Élie Méric, *Le clergé dans l'ancien régime* (Paris: Lecoffre, 1890), 121-129.

3 [Garnier?], 286.

4 Robert Bonfils, archivist of the Jesuit Province of France, explained that, because the Jesuits were suppressed in France, the Jesuit Province of France has virtually no information about the alumni of their college in Tours. Because the college was recognized and supported by the city of Tours, there is some information about the school, most of it legal and financial, at the ADIL. See the ADIL, files on "*Instruction publique*," folders D1 and following.

5 Barnard, 9, tells us that in all there were 562 colleges in France in 1789.

6 A. Lynn Martin, *The Jesuit Mind: The Mentality of an Elite in Early Modern France* (Ithaca, New York: Cornell, 1988), 58.

11

often also enjoyed the support of the local authorities.[7] Boys generally entered a French college at the age of 12 and completed their studies by the age of 17 or 18.[8] So, despite the name "college," these institutions were closer to secondary schools today.

In their colleges the Jesuits stressed the development of the whole person (both knowledge and virtue), the study of languages, including Latin and Greek, and the liberal arts. They did not rely exclusively on lecturing but also employed considerable group work and required the students to do a lot of memorization.

There was also spiritual training at the Jesuit colleges. Daily Mass, regular religious instruction, and monthly confession were required. From early on, the Jesuits in France had a particular devotion to the Blessed Virgin Mary.[9] As a community they also had a deep commitment to the formation of diocesan priests – at the time of their suppression, they had responsibility for thirty-two seminaries in France. So Marian piety and the promotion of priestly vocations were deeply embedded in the culture of the French Jesuit colleges during the *ancien régime*.

This background fits well with what we know about François-Charles Nagot's years as a student of the Jesuits. First, he probably entered the College of Tours in 1743, when he was only about nine, and he spent ten years studying there before he entered the seminary in 1753.[10]

Second, he joined the Sodality of the Blessed Virgin Mary in 1748, when he was fourteen. We are told that he became "one of its most devout members."[11] A "pious association" which arose during the Catholic Reform of the 17th century, this Sodality aimed "by means of the true veneration of the Blessed Virgin, to build up and renew the whole inner man in order to render him capable of and zealous for all works of spiritual love and charity."[12]

---

7 See Dominique Salin. "*La pédagogie jésuite, entre excellence et encouragement*," at http://www.jesuites. com/2014/03/la-pedagogie-jesuite-entre-excellence-et-encouragement/ (accessed 10/11/15). See also Gabriel Cordina, "The '*Modus Parisiensis*,'" (ed.) Vincent J. Duminuco, *The Jesuit Ratio Studiorum: 400th Anniversary Perspectives* (New York: Fordham University Press, 2000), 28-49. In the ADIL (see note 4), there are *Lettres Patentes* (i.e., a published decree) of 1763 that reconfirmed the College of Tours after the departure of the Jesuits. There it indicates that the college was both endowed and subsidized by the city of Tours.

8 Barnard, 9.

9 Martin, 80-81. The French Jesuits renewed their vows annually on the Feast of the Assumption at the church of Notre-Dame-des-Vertus in Paris.

10 Nagot wrote much later that he had been educated by the Jesuits for ten years; so he must have begun his studies with them rather early. See F. C. Nagot, "*Cahier que j'ai commencé d'écrire en 1809*" (Baltimore: handwritten document in Nagot personal papers in the AA, 1809-1812), 7.

11 [Garnier?], 286-287.

12 Anonymous, "Sodality" at http://www.newadvent.org/cathen/14120a.htm (accessed 9/24/15).

Nagot was devoted to the Blessed Virgin Mary and to this Sodality. In 1760, shortly after he was ordained a priest, he would write a note to ask that, at the time of his death, his Certificate of Membership in the Sodality be given to the Jesuit superior of the College of Tours so that the Sodality members there could pray for him. In 1799 he amended this request "with tears" (*"avec larmes"*), stating that his wishes could no longer be fulfilled because the College of Tours was no longer what it was when he was a student there. He ended this amendment by writing a Latin medieval prayer that is used in the Office of the Blessed Virgin Mary:

> Mary Mother of Grace,
> Mother of Mercy,
> Protect us from the enemy,
> Receive us at the hour of our death. [13]

THE VIRGIN IN PRAYER, TOURS, C. 1480
(*MUSÉE DES BEAUX-ARTS DE TOURS*)

---

13 "*Maria Mater Gratiae Mater Misericoridae, Tu nos ab hoste protege, ad hora mortis suscipe.*" He probably learned this prayer at the College of Tours. See his handwritten notes on the back of his Certificate of Enrollment in the Sodality of The Blessed Virgin Mary (Baltimore: printed document in Nagot personal papers in the AA, 1748).

Third, while studying with the Jesuits and like some of their other students, he decided to dedicate his life to the service of the Church. We know this because we have a record of his tonsure on September 26, 1751 by the newly installed Archbishop of Tours Henri-Marie-Bernardin de Rosset de Fleury, grand-nephew of the better-known Cardinal Hercule-André de Fleury whom we shall meet later. Thus Nagot became a cleric at the age of 17.

Fourth and finally, he very likely earned his *maîtrise ès arts* in Tours.[14] In the 18th century, this degree was no longer the major graduate degree that it had been in medieval times. Rather it was merely a certification of the completion of studies in the humanities, or liberal arts, including some philosophy.[15] So it was more like a first college degree today.

---

14 See [Faillon?], "*Notice sur Monsieur*," 1. Faillon wrote that Nagot went to Paris "*au sortir de ses humanités.*" Nagot studied with the Jesuits much longer than necessary to complete his secondary education, and two sources confirm that the College in Tours had professors of theology, philosophy and rhetoric. See Anonymous, *Recueil par ordre de dates, contenant tous les Comptes rendus par MM. les Commissaires du Parlement, au sujet des Collèges, etc.* (Paris: P.G. Simon, 1766). This is also confirmed in the *Lettres Patentes*, or published decree, of 1763. For that document, see note 4, above. In the unlikely event that he received this degree in Paris, it would have been granted by the Sorbonne. See Méric, 142ff.

15 For more information on this degree, see Boris Noguès, "*La maîtrise ès arts en France aux XVIIe et XVIIIe siècles,*" at http://histoire-education.revues.org/2069 (accessed 1/9/16).

The Seminary of Saint Sulpice in Paris

On October 10, 1753, at an age of nineteen, Nagot entered the seminary.[16] The seminary he entered was called the *Robertins,* part of the Sulpician Seminary in Paris. In order to understand the significance of this and of his later assignments in Paris as a Sulpician, it is necessary to know something about the configuration of the Sulpician Seminary there in the 18th century. That institution consisted of four communities, or sub-divisions.[17]

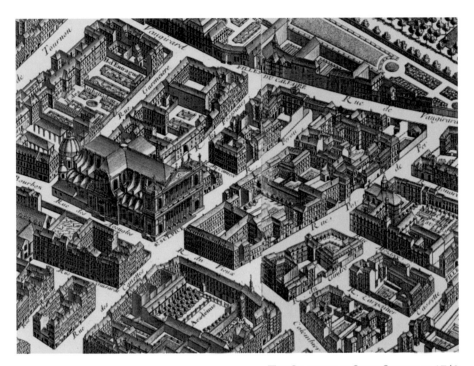

THE SEMINARY OF SAINT SULPICE IN 1740

The first was the *Grand Séminaire,* the program founded by Father Jean-Jacques Olier himself and located in a large building very close to the entrance to the Church of Saint Sulpice.[18] The main entrance to this facility was on the rue

16 See Anonymous, *Catalogue des Messieurs emploiés dans le Séminaire de Saint Sulpice, et dans ceux qui en dépendent* (Paris: handwritten bound volume in the SAP, n.d.), 113.

17 There was also a fifth sub-division, called the Community of Lisieux, or of Laon, but it was not adjacent to the other four sub-divisions.

18 Originally this seminary building had not been so close to the façade of the Church as it was in Father Nagot's day. The new church of Saint Sulpice, finished in 1749 after many decades of construction, was much larger than the medieval church of the same name, and the imposing façade of the new building was much closer to the Seminary.

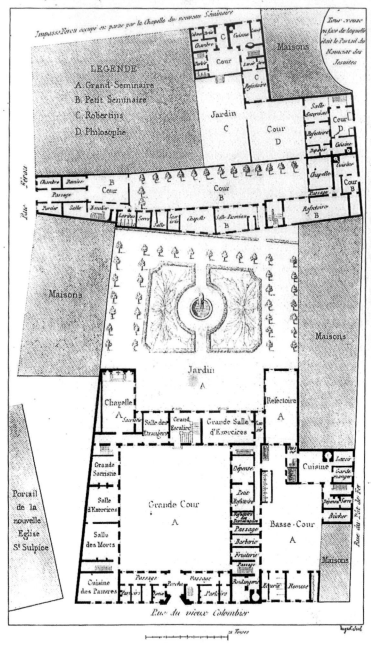

SITE PLAN OF THE SULPICIAN SEMINARY IN PARIS
18TH CENTURY

16

Vieux Colombier, a street that still exists today.[19] This was the program where in the 18th century many young aristocrats from all over France prepared to be priests, shortly afterwards *grands vicaires* (vicars general), and then, most hoped, bishops, archbishops and even cardinals.[20]

Behind the *Grand Séminaire* was a garden and on the other side of the garden was a building called the *Petit Séminaire*.[21] Founded at the end of the 17th century by the Third Superior General Father Louis Tronson (1622-1700), this program was called "*Petit*," not because of the younger age of the seminarians but because of the fact that it charged less than the *Grand Séminaire* and was housed in a less impressive facility.[22] Like the *Grand Séminaire*, the *Petit Séminaire* was also a community of seminarians studying theology.

FATHER TRONSON

The third community that comprised the Sulpician Seminary of Paris was called the Community of Philosophers, or *des Philosophes*. This community, also established by Tronson, was located just behind the *Petit Séminaire* and adjacent to the rue Pot-de-Fer (now the rue Bonaparte). The residents of this community were preparing for the study of theology. So it was a "feeder," so to speak, for the previous two programs.

Finally there was the community of the *Robertins* that Nagot entered in 1753. Named after Father Philippe Robert, one of its early superiors and benefactors, this community was also called the Community of Poor Scholars (*Communauté des pauvres écoliers*), or, more commonly, the Small Community (*Petite-Communauté*). Founded in 1690 and incorporated into the Seminary

---

19 This building, demolished under Napoleon, stood where Saint Sulpice Square (*Place de Saint-Sulpice*) is now located. In the 1820s, it was replaced by a large neo-classical building that faced the Square on the south. That building, confiscated by the government in 1906, is now used as an office of the Center of Public Finance of Paris.

20 John McManners, *Church and Society in Eighteenth-Century France*, I (Oxford: Oxford University, 2003), 228. Most were appointed as *grands vicaires* (vicars general) shortly after ordination. As such, they often ran dioceses for bishops who preferred to live at court or in Paris. According to Gosselin, I, 78, in 1791 more than fifty French bishops were alumni of Saint Sulpice in Paris.

21 The site plan was taken from Jean-Edme-Auguste Gosselin, *Vie de M. Emery, neuvième supérieur du Séminaire et de la Compagnie de Saint-Sulpice,* I (Paris: A. Jouby, 1861). Neither the illustration nor its page are numbered, but it can be found immediately after page 30 of this edition.

22 See, for example, Paguelle de Follenay, *Monsieur Teysseyrre* (Paris: Poussielgue Frère, 1882), 454.

of Saint-Sulpice in 1708, it also occupied buildings behind the *Petit Séminaire* and near the end of a dead-end street called the impasse Férou. Because it was endowed, the program charged very little. It admitted 15 to 18 students per year after rigorous entrance examinations, and many of its seminarians came from urban middle class families from all over France.[23] These seminarians typically began by studying philosophy and then progressed to theology.

So it is fair to say that the internal structure of the Sulpician Seminary in Paris mirrored well the social divisions in contemporary French society that were based on birth and on wealth. In this context, it is also relevant to note that, during the 18th century, Sulpician vocations tended to come from upper class rather than from middle or lower class families.[24] Yet, we know from Nagot's baptismal record that his father was a merchant. We also know that both of his godparents had ties to commerce. So, with the additional fact that he entered the *Robertins* to prepare for priesthood, we can safely conclude that Nagot's family, though not poor, was probably richer in virtue than in possessions.[25]

While Nagot was a seminarian, the quality of the spiritual formation program at the *Grand Séminaire* had been in some decline under the long superior-ship of Father Jean Cousturier, (sometimes Couturier, 1831-70). The main symptoms of this decline were two: many seminarians were not very serious about developing their personal spiritual lives and, accordingly, many were overly

FATHER COUSTURIER

---

23 Gosselin, I, 59. McManners, 330, explains that during the first part of the 18th century most of the parish priests in France came from the urban middle class. The poor could not afford to send their sons to a seminary, and there were few nobles among the parish clergy. Families with bright sons but limited financial resources might aspire to see them admitted into the *Robertins*.

24 Philippe Molac, *Histoire d'un dynamisme apostolique: La Compagnie des prêtres de Saint-Sulpice* (Paris: Cerf, 2008), 58. The translation above is by Lawrence B. Terrien, P.S.S. The families of these Sulpicians were not usually from the highest order of the aristocracy (*noblesse d'épée*, or *de race*) but rather from the lesser aristocracy (*noblesse de robe*) or from the top professional class. It was not until the 19th century that the majority of Sulpicians came from middle class families. Thus, Nagot would have been an atypical Sulpician in the 18th century.

25 Nagot's paternal grandfather Nicholas Nagot is also listed as a merchant, and so his father probably had a head start in business. See the *fichier généalogique* in the AMT.

concerned about their comfort and physical appearance.[26] One historian wrote that things were "far from the original fervor of the time of Jean-Jacques Olier and his early successors."[27]

Problems started to emerge in the 1830s, when Cardinal Hercule-André de Fleury, chief minister of King Louis XV, lived at the Sulpician property in Issy-les-Moulineaux. The seminarians from both the *Grand Séminaire* and *des Philosophes*, many of whom were already ambitious, spent their summer vacations there, and their exposure to the great public figures of France did not improve their motivation.[28]

There were also other causes of the decline at the *Grand Séminaire*. Father Philippe Molac summarized them well in his recent history of the Society of Saint Sulpice:

CARDINAL FLEURY

> The greatest difficulty confronting Father Cousturier was maintaining the quality of priestly formation at the major seminary [*Grand Séminaire*]. The reputation for excellence in the Sulpician formation program at Paris began to attract vocations that were not necessarily well grounded from a spiritual point of view. Consequently, it was becoming more and more difficult to maintain a strict rule of life. The social pressure exercised by the families of the seminarians, most of whom came from the high aristocracy, called into question the ascetical character of certain requirements, especially on the level of personal comfort.[29]

---

26 This period was sometimes called the era of "*frisure*," or curling, because some seminarians spent an excessive amount of time on their coiffure. Many no longer prayed the Rosary or did spiritual reading. See Pierre Boisard, *La compagnie de Saint Sulpice; Trois siècles d'histoire* (Baltimore: a private publication found in the AA, n.d.), 104.

27 "*On est loin de la ferveur primitive du temps de Jean-Jacques Olier et de ses premiers successeurs*." Ibid.

28 "*Malgré toutes ces précautions et les exemples édifiants du cardinal lui-même, sa présence habituelle au séminaire ne laisse pas de nuire beaucoup à la ferveur et à la régularité*." Gosselin, I, 76. A contemporary of Father Nagot wrote that powerful families saw the Sulpician Seminary in Paris as "*le canal des grâces*." See Guillaume-André-René Baston, *Mémoires de l'abbé Baston*, I (Paris: Picard, 1897), 172-173. Abbé Baston also credited the presence of Cardinal Fleury for some of the problems at the Seminary.

29 Molac, 55. See also Baston, 172-173.

Of these aristocratic seminarians, the one best known to history was Charles-Maurice de Talleyrand-Périgord (1754-1838), a young man with an old sterling

pedigree. Charles-Maurice once made the following revelation about his days at the *Grand Séminaire* in the 1770s. He reported that he had a romantic relationship with a woman but noted cynically that those responsible for his formation did not confront him about it because, "'The abbé Cousturier had taught them the art of closing their eyes…and not reproaching a Seminarist [sic] destined for archbishoprics.'"[30,] Complementing Talleyrand's attitude, a standard upper class complaint during the 18th century was that the Sulpicians at the *Grand Séminaire* were obsessed with the minutiae of piety.[31]

TALLEYRAND AS A YOUNG MAN

Despite difficulties at the *Grand Séminaire*, Nagot had a solid formational experience at the *Robertins* because that community had not yet been weakened by the more secular spirit of the *Grand Séminaire*.[32] The students at the *Robertins* tended to come from less privileged families who lived in regions of France where the faith was still taken seriously, i.e., outside the Paris region.

We know a few things about Nagot's years as a seminarian. First, we know that he was a very good student because he was appointed as a *maître des conférences*, a position given to brighter student leaders. To appreciate the significance of this appointment, it is necessary to know a little background.[33] Whatever problems may have existed at the *Grand Séminaire* and, to a lesser extent, at the other

30 McManners, 231. Talleyrand will reappear later in this biography. When elected superior general, Father Cousturier had been made a commendatory abbot ("*abbé*") by Cardinal Fleury, but it was common in the 18th century to refer to all French clerics by this title. The reason was that after tonsure, a cleric was eligible to receive benefices (or ecclesiastical appointments with guaranteed incomes attached), and those whose families had the most influence at court got the most lucrative benefices - they were named commendatory abbots or priors. Eventually, as a courtesy or as a form of flattery, all clerics came to be addressed as "*abbé*."

31 See August Marcade, *Talleyrand: prêtre et évêque* (Paris: Rouveyre et G. Blond, 1883), 18, at http://www.le-prince-de-talleyrand.fr/marcade.pdf (accessed 10/17/2015). See also Louis de Rouvroy, Duc de Saint-Simon, *Memoires de Saint-Simon, nouvelle édition* (Paris: Librarie Hachette et Cie, 1879), 339. See also Dominique Julia, "*L'éducation des ecclésiastiques aux XVIIe et XVIIIe siècles*" in *Problèmes de l'histoire de l'éducation*. (Rome: L'École française de Rome et l'Università di Roma, 1985, 164, at http://www.persee.fr/doc/efr_0000-0000_1988_act_104_1_3271 (accessed 9/12/15).

32 Boisard, 105. See especially Jean-Baptiste Glaire, *Dictionnaire universel des sciences ecclésiastiques*, II (Paris: Poussielgue, 1868), 1970.

33 For a description of this role, see Gosselin, I, 106-107.

programs at the Seminary in Paris, one of them was not a lack of seriousness in regard to academic formation. The seminarians from all divisions attended courses at one of the most prominent local colleges or at the University of Paris, commonly called the Sorbonne. According to one seminarian at that time, the academic review done at the Seminary was more demanding than the classes at the Sorbonne itself.[34] This review was led by the *maîtres des conférences*.

Abbé Guillaume-André-René Baston (1741-1825) was also a *maître des conférences* at Saint Sulpice around Nagot's time. In his *Mémoires* Baston wrote that it was an honor to be chosen for this position and that it came with a stipend. He saw it as a way of learning by teaching others.[35] In light of this last observation, it is likely that Nagot's experience as a *maître de conférences* contributed to his desire to become a Sulpician.

The second thing that we know about Nagot's years in formation at the *Robertins* is that he was a fellow-student of Jacques-André Emery, the future superior general of the Sulpicians who would send him to America in 1791. Emery was a year and a half older than

FATHER BASTON

Nagot and was ordained a priest on March 1, 1758, two years before Nagot. Like Nagot, however, Emery was a very capable student and he too served as a *maître des conférences*.

Third, Nagot's academic program seems to have gone smoothly. After coming to Paris from the College in Tours, he had to study additional philosophy

---

34 McManners, 231.

35 Baston, 172-173. Similarly, from the biography of the later Sulpician Joseph-Laurent Régis Vernet (1760-1843), we learn that a *maître de conférences* was not only responsible for reviewing the material covered in formal lectures but also was closely associated with the faculty of the seminary and thus had some authority over his charges. Vernet saw this experience as a good internship for his later service as a Sulpician. See Nicholas-Joseph Dabert, *Vie de Mr Vernet, Prêtre de Saint-Sulpice* (Lyons: Perisse, 1848), 16-17.

before he could enter the Sorbonne's School of Theology.[36] It was probably in 1756 that Nagot, at the age of 22, enrolled in the Sorbonne where he earned the baccalaureate in theology in 1759.[37] During a seminarian's fourth year of theology at Saint Sulpice, he might begin to study for the licentiate in theology. However, we are told that Nagot did not pursue this degree in Paris because of his frail health and retiring personality.[38]

Fourth, his progress toward priesthood seems to have been very smooth. He was installed as an acolyte on December 17, 1757; ordained a sub-deacon on September 23, 1758; ordained a deacon on December 22, 1759; and ordained a priest for the Archdiocese of Tour on May 31, 1760, by the Archbishop of Paris, Christophe de Beaumont du Repaire (1703-1781).[39]

---

36 We know, for example, from the biography of Abbé Jean-Antoine Nollet that in the 18th century the *maîtrise ès arts* was a prerequisite for the two-year course in philosophy. See Victor-Lucien-Sulpice Lecot, *Abbé Nollet de Pimprez* (Noyon: Couttu-Harlay, 1865), 10. Méric described as follows the reason that the *maîtrise ès arts* was required prior to theology: "*L'étudiant qui entrait ainsi à la Sorbonne, avec l'intention d'explorer le champ vaste et sévère de la théologie, n'était étranger à aucune des sciences connues de son temps; il en connaissait la langue et les éléments, et son esprit ouvert était preparé déjà aux grandes synthèses si chères aux théologiens les plus célèbres du moyen âge.*" Méric, 145.

37 The candidate for the baccalaureate in theology had to be baptized, tonsured and at least 22 years old. He would also have to agree in advance to a three-year program. Méric, 160.

38 [Garnier?], 287. We do not know what his health problem was at this time, and we will see that his health remained poor for some time.

39 Nagot's original certificates of installation and ordination are among his personal papers in the Collection of the Associated Sulpicians of the U.S. at the AA. He probably brought them to the United States in 1791 in order to verify his identity in a place where he was not known.

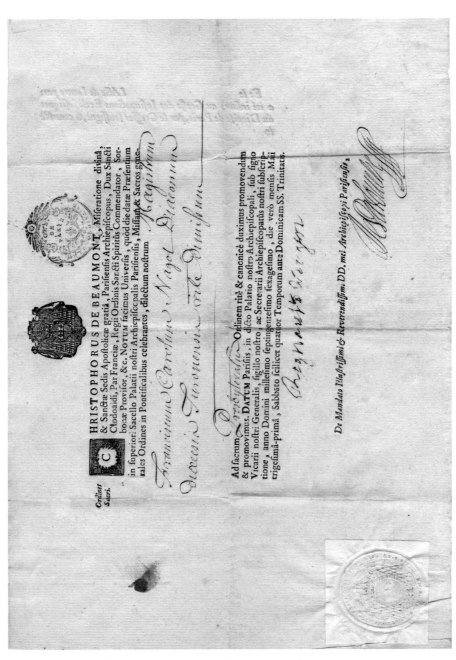

Nagot's Certificate of Ordination to Priesthood

III.

FIRST SULPICIAN ASSIGNMENT:
NANTES (1760-1768)

Archbishop Fleury of Tours gave Nagot permission to join the Sulpicians. So in 1760[1], after attending Solitude, the Sulpician Formation Program, the newly ordained Father Nagot began his first Sulpician assignment at the Seminary of Nantes. [2] Nantes is a small city about 235 miles southwest of Paris and about 125 miles west of Tours, Nagot's birthplace. During the *ancien régime*, the Diocese of Nantes was in the ecclesiastical province of Tours (Rennes did not become an archdiocese until 1859). One of his duties at the Seminary of Nantes was "to teach theology, which obliged him to take the degree of doctor of theology at the University of Nantes with which the seminary was affiliated."[3]

Nagot's study in Nantes seems to have had a serious impact on his thinking. To see this, it is necessary to know about the history of the city. Nantes was the historic seat of the dukes of Brittany and, like most other cities in France, it had a history of religious conflict. Though Brittany was never a major center of French Protestantism, in the early 16th century it did become firmly established in Nantes with the support of some noble families.[4] Nevertheless, the vast majority of the population remained Catholic. By the late-1560s, after the defeat of the Huguenot, or Protestant, forces at the Chateau of Blain, not far from Nantes, Protestant influence in Nantes began to wane.

Nevertheless, later in that century, Nantes was the site of a rebellion against Kings Henri III and Henri IV that was led by the regional governor Philippe-Emmanuel de Lorraine (1558-1602), duke of Mercoeur. Leader of the Holy League (*la sainte ligue*) in Brittany,[5] Mercoeur was opposed to Henri III both because of his perceived leniency toward Protestants and because the king was responsible for the 1588 assassinations of Mercoeur's older brother the Duke of Guise and of his uncle the Cardinal of Lorraine.

---

1 An old list of faculty at the Seminary of Nantes in 1767 indicates that Nagot started there in 1760. The original is in the SAP, Series G, folder 7 G II.

2 Today the seminary is inter-diocesan and is called *Séminaire Saint-Jean de Nantes*. It is housed in a different building from the one it occupied in the 18th century. That earlier building was nationalized during the Revolution and is now a public school.

3 Bertrand, 38. English translation is from *The Voice of the Students and Alumni of St. Mary's Seminary, Baltimore*, XI, no. 7 (April 1934), 19.

4 Yves Durand, ed. *Le Diocèse de Nantes* (Paris: Beauchesne, 1985), 86.

5 The Holy League was a political association that sought to defend Catholicism as the state religion by opposing the power and influence of the French Protestants.

PHILIPPVS EMMANVEL EX LOTHARINGIS,
DVX MERCVRIVS,&c.PAR FRANCIÆ,S.R.I.
PRINCEPS &c.GVBERNATOR BRITANNIÆ.
Anton.Wierx fecit et excudit.

The Duke of Mercour (BnF)

After Henri III's assassination, Mercoeur opposed Henri IV because he was a Huguenot, at least until 1593. Mercoeur may also have sought to rule Brittany as an independent Catholic principality.[6] Though Mercoeur's forces were eventually overcome by the forces of Henri IV in 1598, the Duke's staunchly pro-Catholic policies left a lasting mark on Nantes.

Shortly after Mercoeur's defeat, Henri IV chose Nantes for the signing of his famous act of toleration toward the Huguenots called the Edict of Nantes. It is worth noting that The Edict also reaffirmed Catholicism as the state religion, and this may have contributed to Mercoeur's reconciliation with the king. The Edict marked an end to the religious wars in France.[7] As part of the settlement,

---

6 Brittany had only been fully incorporated into France in 1532, and it is said that Mercoeur named his son both Duke and Prince of Brittany. But some see no evidence that Mercoeur wanted to undo the union with France. See, e.g, Malcolm Walsby, *The Printed Book in Brittany 1484-1600* (Leiden: Brill, 2011), 214. There are different opinions about the relative importance of religion as a motivating factor in the Guise family.

7 It did not end conflict between Catholics and Protestants in France.

HENRI IV

the number of Huguenot places of worship in Nantes was reduced to less than three.[8]

During the 17th century, Nantes, like many other cities in France, experienced an intense renewal of Catholicism. The spirit of the Holy League was still in evidence, and the influence of the Huguenots continued to decline. In 1670 it was said that the people there remained "deeply devout and Catholic until death".[9] In this context, it is also important to recall that it was in 1685 that King Louis XIV revoked the Edict of Nantes, leading many Huguenots to leave France and some others to convert or at least to consider conversion.

By the time Nagot arrived in Nantes in 1760, the city's strong economy depended heavily on trade, especially the French slave trade. Nantes was also full of religious houses, including those of the Dominicans, the Carmelites,

---

8 Durand, 90.

9 "[They were] *fort pieux et catholique jusqu'à la mort*." Ibid., 128.

TRUTH UNMASKS HERESY, 1686 (BNF)

the Franciscans, the Ursulines, the Jesuits, the Visitandines, and the Christian Brothers. The city had its own diocesan seminary and an organization dedicated to the continuing formation of priests.[10]

During the next few years, Nagot served at the Seminary while pursuing graduate studies in dogmatic theology at the University of Nantes. Founded in 1460, this University had five faculties, or schools, of which the most important were law, medicine and theology. Its chancellor was the bishop of Nantes. An expert

---

10 This organization for continuing formation, called the Community of St. Clement, had been founded in 1671 by Father René Lévêque, a student of Father Olier.

on the history of the University has written that to attain the doctorate in theology could take up to 15 years of study.[11] In Nagot's case, however, the program took only a few years because he had already earned the *maîtrise ès arts* and the baccalaureate in theology.

We do not know anything specific about his course of studies at the University of Nantes. We do know a fair amount, however, about a recent conflict involving the theology faculty there. In 1625 the Oratorians had established a very successful school in Nantes called the College of Saint Clement. Gradually this community gained control over the faculty of theology of the University. By the early 18th century, many professors were partial to the teachings of the Jansenist Oratorian Pasquier Quesnel (1634-1719).[12] In 1713, at the urging of King Louis XIV, Pope Clement XI issued the apostolic constitution, or bull, entitled *Unigenitus Dei Filius* condemning some of Quesnel's teachings. However, the faculty of theology rejected the bull, much to the disapproval of the local Bishop, Gilles-Jean-François de Beauvau du Rivau (1652-1717).

SEAL OF THE FACULTY OF THEOLOGY IN NANTES

FATHER QUESNEL (BNF)

---

11 Yves Durand, "*La faculté de théologie de Nantes,*" Ch. III of Gérard Emptoz, ed. *Histoire de l'université de Nantes, 1460-1993.* (Rennes: Presses Universitaires de Rennes, 2002), 49. First the typical candidate had to earn the *maîtrise ès arts*, signifying competency in the humanities. After about five more years of study, he would earn the baccalaureate in theology. This would qualify him to pursue the licentiate in theology, a program that would normally take two or three more years. Finally the doctorate could be attained after a few more requirements and formalities. McManners, 229, explains that in the 18th century the licentiate was the critical degree for ecclesiastical advancement and that, after the licentiate, one could earn the doctorate fairly easily, though few did.

12 A movement within Catholicism, Jansenism was named after Cornelius Jansen, Bishop of Ypres (1585-1638). After Jansen's death, some of his ideas on grace and human nature were condemned by the Church but they became widespread nevertheless. Jansenism was strongly critical of much Jesuit theology, especially Molinism, and it was socially divisive in France. So it was strongly opposed by Louis XIV.

There ensued a protracted struggle between the bishops of Nantes and the faculty of theology. It was only resolved when Beauvau's successor, Bishop Louis de La Vergne-Montenard du Tressan (1670-1733), obtained a *lettre de cachet,* or an order over the royal seal, that allowed him to purge the faculty of theology.[13] After that, the influence of Jansenism and of the Oratorians declined at the University.[14] By the time Nagot studied there, the University's faculty of theology was seen as orthodox.

So we can see that Nantes, like other university-cities in France, was a site of much theological controversy during the *ancien régime.* We have also seen that its name will forever be associated with the insecure fate of Protestants in France. This history provides a necessary context for appreciating Nagot's strong interest in nurturing and spreading the Catholic faith, themes that would become prominent in his later life and writing.[15]

We also know some relevant facts about the history of the seminary in Nantes.[16] It had been founded by Father Jean-Jacques Olier in 1649 at the request of Bishop Gabriel de Beauvau de Rivarennes (d.1668), great uncle of Bishop Beauvau de Rivau, above.[17] Before then, the Oratorians had been assisting with the preparation of young men for the priesthood, and so the Oratorians were annoyed when Beauvau de Rivarennes entrusted his new seminary to the Sulpicians. At first, their annoyance, along with a

BEAUVAU FAMILY ARMS

lack of available personnel, caused Olier to hesitate – he had a great respect for the Oratorians, the sons of Cardinal Bérulle and Father Condren. However, Beauvau insisted that he wanted the Sulpicians, and no other community, to take charge.[18]

In 1660, however, much to the disappointment of Beauvau, the Sulpicians withdrew from the seminary due to a tangle of local problems, including poor financial support and a serious conflict with the vicar general who had direct oversight of the seminary.[19]

---

13 The issuance of *lettres de cachet* was a feature of royal absolutism. By their authority an innocent person could be imprisoned without a hearing. Beauvau's *lettre* enabled him to override the normal privileges of the professors at the University since they could not appeal such a royal ordinance.

14 See J. Mouille, *Histoire du Grand Séminaire de Nantes* (Paris: typed manuscript in the SAP, n.d.), 81.

15 Nagot's focus was probably encouraged by Father Olier's emphasis on evangelization.

16 One of Father Olier's benefices was the Priory of Clisson in the Diocese of Nantes.

17 The later Beauvau was also the nephew of his immediate predecessor Bishop Gilles de la Baume le Blanc de la Valiere. This illustrates that some benefices were kept in the family during the *ancien regime*: one family member would resign "in favor of" another.

18 Mouille, 23-24.

19 Ibid., 38. While the bishop expressed deep sorrow about the loss of the Sulpicians, it was noted at the time that the bishop did nothing significant to redress their grievances.

As we have already seen, more than forty years later, Beauvau's grandnephew Gilles de Beauvau du Rivau was serving as bishop of Nantes when the faculty of theology at the University rejected *Unigenitus*. As part of his response, this later Beauvau began to have the seminarians take some of their courses at the seminary itself.[20] Yet those courses too became tainted with Jansenism, and tension grew between the bishops of Nantes and the faculty of the seminary.

This tension was finally put to rest by Bishop Christophe-Louis Turpin de Cressé de Sanzay (1670-1745). In 1728, after long negotiations with the Superior General of Saint Sulpice, he managed to have the entire faculty of the Seminary replaced with Sulpicians in order to ensure orthodoxy in the training of his priests.[21] Naturally this decision also contributed to the decline of the influence of Jansenism in Nantes. By 1730 the leadership of the church in Nantes was largely in orthodox hands.[22]

By the time Nagot arrived in Nantes in 1760, it was a place where the Sulpicians were thriving. The Seminary was graduating 20-25 students each year,[23] and the region was the source of many Sulpician vocations. When Nagot arrived, the local superior was

BISHOP MUSANACHÈRE

---

20 Ibid., 72. The same thing happened in Angers, and Professor Dominique Julia has argued recently that the "one-roof" seminary (where academic formation is internal to the institution) got a strong impetus from this. Moreover, he believes that, as a result, the philosophical and theological education of clerics suffered. See his *"L'éducation des ecclésiastiques aux XVIIe et XVIIIe siècles,"* 147. Julia also points out that about the same time the Sulpicians began to review the notes of their students to make sure that they were getting orthodox theology. Ibid. 172.

21 See L. Lucas, *"Deux interessantes thèses de l'histoire locale,"* in *L'Ouest-Eclair,* Aug. 25, 1934, 4- 5. This is a summary of two important works on the history of the Church in Nantes that were published by Canon Alcime Bachelier (1888-1962) as part of his doctoral work. One of these was published as Alcime Bachelier, *Le Jansénisme à Nantes* (Anger: Imprimerie de l'Anjou, 1934; also Paris: Nizet et Bastard, 1934). In an earlier related article, Bachelier wrote, *"De ce jour la cause de Jansénisme à Nantes était perdue. Les fils de M. Olier - de tous les religieux - étaient peut-être les seuls à pouvoir engager la bataille avec la certitude de vaincre,"* Alcime Bachelier, *"Le Jansénisme à Nantes de 1714 à 1728"* in *Mémoires de la société d'histoire et d'archéologie de Bretagne,* X (1929), 55-56.

22 Durand, "La faculté," 57. Later a Jansenist publication called these events *"une vengeance **Sulpicienne**"* [sic]." Mouille, 103. This was certainly not the first conflict between Jansenism and the Sulpicians. See Kauffman, 18-21. See also John McManners, *French Ecclesiastical Society under the Ancien Regime* (Manchester, UK: 1970), 13.

23 See Anonymous, *"Un peu d'histoire,"* at http://seminaire-nantes.cef.fr/un-peu-dhistoire/ (accessed on 8/6/15). See also Durand, *Le Diocèse de Nantes,* 149.

Father Claude Rouhier who had already been in that position for eight years but who was not well and so relied on one of his confreres, Father Pierre Féris (1719-1788) to assist in running the institution.[24] In 1762 Rouhier died, and his former right-hand-man was named superior. Féris had been at the seminary since 1745 and because he remained as superior until 1788, he brought great stability to the seminary.[25] Féris also enjoyed a cordial relationship with the then Bishop of Nantes Pierre Mauclerc de la Musanchère, and was a vicar general of the diocese. So Nagot was fortunate to have his critical first assignment as a Sulpician in a stable institution with an experienced rector during a period of very warm diocesan relations.

Based on a narrative left by a 1770 alumnus of that seminary, we know that the daily schedule in the 1760s was very similar to the one that Nagot knew from his years in Paris. The horarium in Nantes was as follows:[26]

5:00 a.m.	Rising
5:30 a.m.	Meditation and community prayer
6:15 a.m.	Community Mass
8:15 a.m.	Breakfast
8:45 a.m.	Classes and study
11:15 a.m.	Particular examen
11:30 a.m.	Lunch, followed by one hour of recreation
1:00 p.m.	Vespers
1:30 p.m.	Classes
5:15 p.m.	Matins and the office of the day
6:00 p.m.	Spiritual reading
6:30 p.m.	Supper followed by recreation
8:30 p.m.	Compline and bedtime

The schedule was different on Sundays and major feast days, and three times a week there were conferences in the first part of the morning, often on matters

---

24 For more information about Féris, see Bertrand, I, 426-431. We know that Nagot's other confreres in Nantes were: Julien Salver (1723-1781), Jean-Baptiste Denans (1717-1783), and René-Michel Mirlau (probably a young non-Sulpician). So, as expected, Nagot was one of the youngest.

25 Mouille, 106-107.

26 Mouille, 115ff. The time for Vespers seems especially strange. At Saint Sulpice in Paris, one old source says that Matins and Lauds were at 4:45 p.m. for those obliged to say the breviary. Vespers was, more naturally, in the evening. See Anonymous, *Réglement Général du Séminaire de Saint Sulpice [à Paris]* (Paris: bound calligraphic manuscript in the SAP, n.d.), sections X and XIII.

covered in academic courses. The rosary was usually recited privately.[27]

As we have already seen, the second Bishop Beauvau had moved the teaching of some courses to the seminary when the University's School of Theology became tainted with Jansenism. This arrangement was codified in 1724 by *lettres patentes*, or a published legal proclamation.[28] According to that document, two kinds of courses were to be taught at the seminary. The first were courses in dogmatic, or scholastic, theology, and the second were courses in moral theology. Those who taught these courses were supposed to have doctorates and to be accepted into the University's Faculty of Theology. So Nagot had to earn the licentiate and the doctorate so that he would be fully qualified to teach.

It was during his time in Nantes that we get our first glimpse into François-Charles Nagot the priest. Starting in 1767, and continuing until 1770, shortly after he had left Nantes, he wrote a series of letters in reply to those of a young man whom he addressed as *"M. l'abbé Curatteau"*.[29] From the content and tone of these letters, Nagot was probably his spiritual director at the Seminary of Nantes.[30] It seems that Curatteau was struggling with doubts about his vocation because of his academic limitations and also because of some physical ailment affecting his legs. Father Nagot's caring letters expressed sincere sympathy and contained promises to pray for him. Nevertheless, Nagot also gave some clear advice: "Neglect neither study nor prayer, in such a state of mind." And he offered Curatteau a challenge that would prove prophetic both for Curatteau and for Nagot himself: "It should cost us something to arrive at the incomparable dignity of priesthood; and once arrived there, it must cost us even more to faithfully fulfill the plans of God and to satisfy our duties both towards God and towards our brothers, whose salvation is, so to speak, in our hands."[31] Curatteau apparently took these words to heart and struggled on to ordination as a priest.

---

27 In Paris the day seems to have begun a bit later, and the Rosary was recited in common in the late afternoon before spiritual reading (to ensure that the more secularized seminarians prayed it). Community Mass was at 7:00 a.m. in the summer and 7:30 a.m. in the winter. See *"Ordre du jour,"* in *"Règlement 1769"* (Paris: handwritten document in the file entitled, *"Anciens Règlement"* in the SAP, 1769).

28 Mouille, 123ff

29 Nagot's addressing him as "M. l'abbé" would not have precluded his still being a seminarian. See Ch. II, n. 30

30 Based on these letters, we know that around 1770 Curatteau (sometimes Curateau) was somehow associated with the church or chapel of Notre-Dame de Bonsecours in Nantes, a building that no longer exists as it was prior to the French Revolution. It seems that he was related to the older and more famous Jean-Baptiste Curatteau (1729-1790), a Sulpician from Nantes who was well known in Montreal as the founder of the Collège de Montréal. Our Curratteau was apparently Jean-Baptiste's half-brother René. (Jean-Baptiste's uncle Claude was also a priest but he died in 1765.) See P. Grégoire, *État de diocèse de Nantes en 1790* (Nantes: Forest & Grimaud, 1882), 49. See also J.-Bruno Harel, *"Curatteau, John Baptiste"* at http://www.biographi.ca/en/bio/curatteau_jean_baptiste_4E.html (accessed on 8/4/15).

31 Nagot, François-Charles, Letters to Abbé Curatteau, trans. R. MacDonough (Baltimore: four handwritten documents in Nagot correspondence in the AA, 1767-70).

During the French Revolution two decades later, unrest among Catholics and royalists in the region just south of Nantes led to what is called the War of the Vendée *(Guerre de Vendée)*, the most violent part of which took place from 1793 until 1796. Early in that conflict, the brutal revolutionary official John-Baptiste Carrier executed everyone in Nantes who was deemed sympathetic to the rebels. Thousands, including hundreds of priests, were drowned in the Loire in what was euphemistically called "verticle deportation."[32] Among Carrier's victims was Curatteau who put loyalty to his faith and his vocation above loyalty to the demands of the revolutionary government.[33]

Unfortunately, while in Nantes, Nagot's health became a serious concern. When it began to interfere with his teaching, he was called back to Paris.[34]

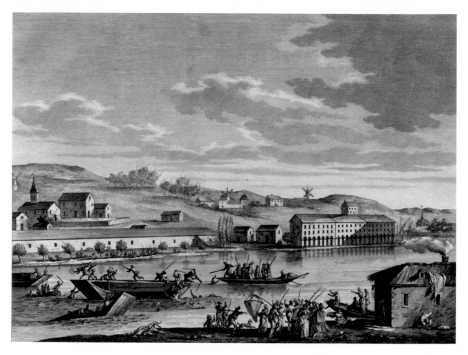

DROWNINGS AT NANTES (BNF)

---

32 See LeNotre, *Les noyades de Nantes* (Paris: Perrin, 1912), 150. See also Gomez-Le Chevanton, Corinne. *Carrier et la Révolution française* (Nantes: Geste, 2004), 23.

33 Carrier executed Curateau and 89 other imprisoned non-juring, or recusant, priests in the First Drowning on November 16-17, 1793. The list of victims includes, *"Curateau René (sacriste Saint-Denis de Nantes)."* See, e.g., Anonymous, *"Etymologie et Histoire de Nantes,"* See also note 4 at Anonymous, *Etymologie et histoire de Nantes,"* at http://www.infobretagne.com/nantes.htm (accessed 8/12/15).

34 [Garnier?], 287. Nagot's illness at the time is not specified.

IV

LEADERSHIP OF THE *ROBERTINS*
(1769-1781)

In 1768, Nagot, at the age of 35, arrived in Paris where his health began to improve.[1] For the next 22 years, he seemed to remain reasonably healthy while he held important leadership positions at the premier Sulpician Seminary in France.

He arrived in Paris shortly before the death of Father Cousturier on March 31, 1770, and he would serve there under three other superiors general. The first was Father Claude Bourachot (1770-1777) who was discouraged by his failure to reform the *Grand Séminaire*.[2] The second was Father Pierre Le Gallic (1777-1782) whose acerbic personality thwarted his good intentions during a very brief tenure.[3] The third and most important was Nagot's contemporary Father Jacques-André Emery (1782-1811), a priest of extraordinary ability and determination, whose success at reform was cut short by the French Revolution.

LOUIS XV

Before discussing Father Nagot's two decades of ministry in France's capital, it is important to review some concurrent political and economic developments that would eventually alter the course of his life. On May 10, 1774 King Louis XV died at Versailles after a reign of sixty years. By the end of his life, he was quite unpopular. A key reason for this was his entanglement in fruitless foreign wars, especially the disastrous Seven Years War (1756-1763), called the French and Indian War in North America. It was a very costly undertaking for France both politically and financially. On the political side, France lost its colony of New France in North America to Great Britain.[4] This loss was an enormous blow to French prestige. On the financial side, the War forced the French treasury to add to its already huge national debt.

---

1 In 1767 he wrote to Currateau that he was recovering little by little. In 1770 he wrote that his health was "good enough" ("*assez bonne*") and "much better than before" ("*beaucoup meilleure que ci-devant*"). It seems, nevertheless, that Nagot had a weak constitution and he suffered a lot from it during his later years, as we will see below.

2 Boisard, 111-112.

3 Gosselin, I, 100-101. Father Le Gallic resigned in 1782, creating a need for an extraordinary general assembly.

4 This colony included Montreal where the Sulpicians had served for more than a century.

The Marquis de Condorcet

As Louis XV's fortunes were declining, a group of French intellectuals who spoke for many in the rising middle class were beginning to call for reform of the entire system in France, including abolishing the remnants of feudalism and curtailing the power of the monarchy, the nobility, and the Church. In general, these intellectuals, called philosophes, used reasoned arguments against traditional practices that they considered indefensible.[5] Some of these writers were empiricists, deists, and atheists. Among the philosophes were skilled authors like Charles-Louis de Montesquieu (1689-1755), Voltaire (1694-1788), Jean-Jacques Rousseau (1712-1778), and Denis Diderot (1713-1784). As the last philosophe the Marquis de Condorcet would describe them in 1793, "A class of men speedily made their appearance in Europe whose object was less to discover and investigate truth, than to disseminate it; who, pursuing prejudice through all the haunts and asylums in which the clergy, the schools, governments and privileged corporations had placed and protected it, made it their glory rather to eradicate popular errors than add to the stores of human knowledge."[6]

The ideas of the philosophes were widely disseminated among the well-educated, especially in the salons of Paris, during the second half of the 18th century. Their case for reform was also digested in many popular pamphlets. These ideas fueled a growth of skepticism and led to a relaxation of moral standards, especially among the better educated members of French society. [7] Moreover, the appeal of this movement forced the Church into a largely defensive intellectual posture.[8,]

In 1774, when Louis XV was succeeded by his grandson Louis XVI, the new king faced huge challenges ("*le déluge*"), including weak public support for the monarchy and a mountain of debt. Louis XVI was not a strong leader

---

5 In *Émile*, Rousseau wrote the following about reforming education in France, "'Take the very reverse of the current custom and you will nearly always do right.'" Barnard, 18.

6 Antoine-Nicolas de Condorcet, *Outlines of an Historical View of the Progress of the Human Mind*, trans. anonymous (Chicago: G. Langer, 2009), 275-276.

7 After 1750, other signs of growing secularization or de-Christianization were seen among the urban population. See Timothy Tackett, "The French Revolution and Religion to 1794," in *The Cambridge History of Christianity*, VI, eds. S. Brown and T. Tackett (Cambridge, UK: Cambridge University Press, 2006), 539.

8 In this context, it is interesting to note that the seminarians at Saint Sulpice in Paris read some of the works of the philosophes so that they could learn how to refute them. See Baston, 59. Baston attended the *Robertins*.

LOUIS XVI

and he had recently married Marie
Antoinette, an Austrian grand
duchess who eventually became quite
unpopular, even despised, because

Marie-Antoinette

of her extravagant lifestyle and her opposition to reform. This factor further
diminished the public standing of the monarchy.

Moreover, in the late 1770s the new King allowed France to get into another
expensive foreign venture by supporting the American colonials against France's
old enemy Great Britain.[9] This aid was given during a period of economic
decline in France, and so eventually the king was forced to seek novel sources
of revenue. This would play an important role in the outbreak of the French
Revolution as we shall see later.

While these important developments were taking place, Nagot's energy, for the
most part, was absorbed by his duties inside the Sulpician Seminary in Paris.
First, shortly after he arrived in Paris in 1768,[10] he was named superior of the
Robertins, his own alma mater.[11] By then, that program was known as "the
community where the most brilliant, most promising, young ecclesiastics were
united."[12] He remained superior there for 12 years.

---

9 Benjamin Franklin, a representative of the Continental Congress to France, arrived at Nantes on
December 7, 1776, and started an arduous but ultimately effective effort to draw France into the War.

10 There is a letter to Abbé Currateau addressed from Paris and dated June 21, 1768.

11 His obituary puts this appointment in 1769. See [Garnier?], 287. Late in his life, Nagot wrote that
he never wanted to be a superior, but obviously his superiors over many years saw qualities in him that
recommended him for leadership.

12 Annabelle Melville, *Louis William DuBourg* (Chicago: Loyola University Press, 1986), 17.

From several sources, we know that Father Nagot's leadership of the *Robertins* was very effective. According to a later summary:

> He gently corrected abuses that crept in under a less firm administration, he improved the temporal administration of the house, he encouraged studies, he formed a library,[13] and he devoted himself especially to the establishment of regularity and fervor in the house. The *Petite Communauté*, under his direction, gave doctors to the Sorbonne, *grand vicaires* to several diocèses, [and] apostles to China and Tonquin.[14]

Another testimony to his success can be found in a letter of April 9, 1816, written by the then Superior General Father Antoine du Pouget Duclaux (1749-1827). Duclaux wrote, "It was my privilege to be trained by him during my years of study at the Little Community [i.e., the *Robertins*], and I can guarantee that that house has had few superiors more capable than he in maintaining there the spirit of piety and regularity which must characterize all seminaries."[15]

We also have a more personal story about Nagot that was left by one of his former students at the *Robertins*, Jean de Brumauld de Beauregard (1749-1841), a future bishop of Orleans. Later in life Beauregard described Nagot as "a courageous man, a good man, and a man as devout as an angel."[16] In this context Beauregard recalled the following curious encounter that took place in the late 1770s. One of his friends, Gaspard de Cambis, future vicar general of Chartres and chaplain of the queen of France, was unnerved by a seemingly insignificant incident that had taken place while he was giving religious instruction to children. He went to Beauregard who was the student in charge of the program of religious instruction, and Beauregard took him to Nagot. When they arrived, Nagot

---

13 The establishment of the library was also mentioned in some recollections of Abbé Mercier de Saint-Léger (1734-1799), a librarian in Paris from 1760-1772 and a contemporary of Nagot. Perhaps Nagot consulted him on the project. See "*Souveniers de l'abbé de St. Léger,*" in *Matériaux pour la vie de Monsieur Emery*, 4 (Paris: bound volume in the SAP, n.d.), 426.

14 "*Il corrigea doucement les abus qui s'étoient glissés sous une administration moins ferme, améliora le temporel de la maison, encouragea les études, forma une bibliothèque, et s'appliqua surtout à établir la régularité et la ferveur dans la maison. La petite communauté, sous sa conduite, donna des docteurs à la Sorbonne, des grands vicaires à plusieurs diocèses, des apotres à la Chine et au Tonquin.*" [Garnier?], 287. Tonquin, or Tonkin, is the name of the northern part of the Kingdom of Annam, very roughly today's Vietnam, just south of China. A Catholic hierarchy was established in the region in the 17th century, when Father Olier himself volunteered to go as a missionary either to Tonquin or to Cochin China (the southern part of the Kingdom of Annam). See Edward H. Thompson, *The Life of Jean-Jacques Olier, Founder of the Seminary of Saint Sulpice*, new and enlarged ed. (New York: Burns & Oates, 1886), 536-537.

15 Vincent M. Eaton, ed. and trans., *Necrology of the Society of Saint Sulpice, Province of the U.S.* (unpublished bound text in the AA, n.d.), 5. Antoine du Pouget Duclaux (1749-1827) began as a seminarian at the *Robertins* in 1770 and completed his doctorate in 1778. So he was there for most of Nagot's time as superior.

16 "*M. Nagot Supérieur des Robertins était un brave homme, un bon homme, il était pieux comme un ange,*" See "*Souvenirs de Mgr. B. de Beauregard*", in *Matériaux*, 4, 175.

was busy polishing the steps of his personal altar. Beauregard said to him, "I present to you my disturbed friend." Nagot replied in Latin: "*Ego autem scopebam spiritum meum*, i.e., literally, "But I was searching my spirit."[17] This was a paraphrase of Psalm 77, verse 7, that reads, ["I ponder and] my spirit broods."

BISHOP BEAUREGARD

What was Nagot saying to the two seminarians that made his words so memorable for one of them? It is possible that Nagot was putting them off by indicating that he was meditating or in prayer while tidying up the place where he celebrated Mass. A more natural interpretation would be that, when he saw the expression on the face of young Gaspard de Cambis, he used some familiar words from a psalm of lament to offer a kind of scriptural diagnosis: Gaspard was clearly brooding over something. In either case, this story illustrates how familiar Nagot was with the scriptures. He used scripture verses to interpret events and he often included them, as asides, in his letters and informal writings. It was said much later that he had "a singular attraction to holy scripture which he read and meditated on constantly."[18]

During his time of leadership at the *Robertins*, Nagot maintained ties with his family, visiting his parents in Tours during some of his vacations.[19] In the summer of 1779, he asked the general council to provide a small annual pension to his father (Bernard Nagot) who was old and in need of assistance.[20] The request was granted gladly ("*volontiers*") at a meeting of the general council on July 3, 1779.[21]

---

17 These words were based on the Vulgate's translation of Psalm 76: 7.

18 [Garnier?], 288.

19 See, for example, The Minutes of the General Council, meeting of Aug. 1, 1771 (Paris: Handwritten bound volume in the SAP, Manuscript 23, III, 209.

20 Since his parents had been married in 1728, his father must have been around seventy at that time.

21 The Minutes of the General Council, III, July 3, 1779, (Paris: bound volume in the SAP), 359.

V

LEADERSHIP OF THE *PETIT SÉMINAIRE*
(1781-1789)

Because of Nagot's great success at the *Robertins*, in 1781, Le Gallic named him, at the age of 47, as superior of the *Petit Séminaire,* a position he would hold for the next eight years. It was during this period that we learn more about him and his priorities as a Sulpician.

We are given some information by biographers of Louis-Guillaume-Valentin DuBourg (1766-1833), a future bishop and another of his seminarians who worked closely with him both in France and in the U.S. Born in the French island-colony of Haiti (called Saint-Domingue at the time), DuBourg was the son of a successful planter and merchant. At an early age he was sent back to Bordeaux for his education. On October 12, 1786, he entered the *Petit Séminaire* under Nagot's leadership. "In him Mr. DuBourg found a master worthy of his promising talents and piety; soon he enjoyed all his affection and confidence."[1] During those years, Nagot was perhaps the most important influence on him;[2] DuBourg admired Nagot because of his "success and his exemplary piety."[3] We will see much more of DuBourg later.

There is also a personal tribute to Nagot at this time that came from Guy-Toussaint-Julien Carron (1760-1821), a priest of the Diocese of Rennes. It was said that Carron led such a holy life that some called him the "*Abbé Thé*rèse"[4] and that he was so devoted to the poor that others called him the "'Vincent de Paul of our days.'"[5] Carron must have studied at Saint Sulpice in Paris where he was

FATHER CARRON

---

1 Anonymous, "Archbishop DuBourg," in *Jesuit, or, Catholic Sentinel,* No. XIX (May 10, 1834), 147-148, at http://newspapers.bc.edu/cgi-bin/bostonsh?a=d&d=jcsthree18340510-01.2.4 (accessed Oct. 10, 2015).

2 Melville, 22.

3 "*À cause de ses succès et de sa piété examplaire.*" See the biography of Archbishop DuBourg of Besançon in François Xavier de Feller, *Biographie universelle,* II (Besançon: Outhenin-Chalandre, 1838), 618.

4 James Roosevelt Bayley, *The Life of Simon William Gabriel Bruté* (London: Burns & Oates, n.d.), 4. Carron was the first spiritual director of the Sulpician Simon Bruté (1779-1839) and had a profound effect on him.

5 James Roosevelt Bayley, *Memoirs of the Right Reverend Simon Wm. Bruté, D.D., First Bishop of Vincennes* (New York: J. S. Shea, 1860), 13.

influenced by Nagot.[6] A few years after Nagot's death, in a published challenge to priests who allowed themselves to be distracted from their ministry by secular interests, Carron presented Nagot as a model and wrote the following somewhat cryptic invocation:

> O Virtuous Nagot, in the early years of my priesthood I too reaped the harvest of your inexhaustible charity: charged to plead, before the charitable inhabitants of the city, the cause of my miserable fellow citizens, O man of God, I never invoked without success your influence that served me as an eloquent advocate.[7]

During this period, Nagot also demonstrated some of his priorities as a Sulpician. First, he worked closely with Father Emery, the superior general as of 1782, to tighten up the program at the *Petit Séminaire*. Though the program there was more solid than the one at the *Grand Séminaire*, some of the malaise of the latter had begun to spread to the former.[8] One of Nagot's students at the time, Philippe-François Sausin (1756-1844), future bishop of Blois, confirmed that Nagot reinvigorated the community, and Sausin remembered Nagot as devout and a man of prayer. Seminarians saw him as one of the best spiritual directors at Saint Sulpice.[9] Sausin also recalled that Nagot was a good speaker and that one day he gave a homily during a retreat in which he used such a powerful image that the entire community was struck by his words.[10]

FATHER EMERY AS SUPERIOR GENERAL

---

6 Carron's tribute was presented in the form of a footnote to a passage that described Nagot's accomplishments in Paris.

7 "*Vertueux Nagot, et moi aussi dans la jeunesss [sic] de mon Sacerdoce, je recueillis les fruits de ton inépuisable charité: chargé de plaider, auprès des habitants charitables de la métropole, la cause de mes malheureux concitoyens, homme de Dieu, je n'invoquai point sans succés, ton crédit qui devint pour moi comme un avocat éloquent.*" Carron, 179. During the Revolution, Carron was imprisoned and then exiled to the island of Jersey, a British territory, where he became famous for his service to other French exiles in Britain.

8 "*[I]l en fut tiré, en 1780, pour être mis à la tête du petit séminaire, qui était alors un peu déchu de sa régularité, et qui lui fut aussi redevable d'un renouvellement sensible dans sa ferveur.*" Bertrand, 38. See also Boisard, 140.

9 "*Souvenirs de Mgr. de Sausin*", in *Matériaux* , 4, 120.

10 The image was a skillful comparison between the process used in composing Diderot's famous *Encyclopédie* and the construction process used for the Tower of Babel. Ibid.

Nagot also demonstrated his commitment to sound spiritual formation by re-editing and republishing in 1784 a popular book on prayer, *Instructions familières sur l'oraison mentale*, written by Abbé Noël Courbon in 1685.[11] It seems likely that he did this for the benefit of the seminarians under his care.

After the publication of Courbon's book, Nagot translated into French an English work by one of his recent seminarians John Thayer (1755-1818).[12] This was an account of Thayer's conversion to Catholicism.[13] Nagot's translation, which included more stories of conversions in later editions, proved quite popular in France, and it was also published in Quebec and translated into other languages.[14] It was further expanded and republished several times during the following decades.[15]

Thayer was descended from an old New England Puritan family and had been a well-known Congregationalist minister. During a visit to Italy in 1783, he was converted. After a year at the College of Navarre in Paris, Thayer entered the *Petit Séminaire* on October 18, 1784. He was ordained a priest in Paris on the day before Trinity Sunday in 1787 and soon became a controversial figure in the early history of the Church in the U.S.[16]

Nagot had much admiration for Thayer during his seminary days because of his strong piety, likely a result of his recent conversion. For example, Nagot praised him for making a pilgrimage to the Basilica of Saint Martin of Tours just prior to his departure from France in order to seek the Saint's blessing.[17] Thayer's evident piety, along with that of another seminarian-convert Pierre-Mathieu-

---

11 Bertrand, 42.

12 See the Bibliography. This is the first time that we have evidence that Nagot could read English. When he learned it we do not know. Moreover, as we shall see shortly, Thayer was not the only native English-speaker with whom Nagot had communication prior to his arrival in the U.S.

13 John Thayer, *An Account of the Conversion of the Reverend Mr. John Thayer, Lately a Protestant Minister, at Boston in North-America, who Embraced the Roman Catholic Religion at Rome, on the 25th of May, 1783* (London: Goddard, 1788). Nagot's original translation was entitled, *Relation de la conversion de quelques Protestans.* (Paris: Prevôt et Crapart, 1789). When Benjamin Franklin heard of Thayer's conversion, he said that our ancestors had gone from Catholic to Anglican to Presbyterian; so Thayer, by going to "popery," seemed to be going backwards. See Benjamin Franklin, *Writings of Benjamin Franklin*, IX, ed. A. Smythe (New York: Haskell House, 1970), 303.

14 See, e.g., *Narratio conversionis J. Thayer.* trans. M. Hublot (Munster, unnamed publisher, 1794).

15 Recently Michèle Sàcquin pointed out that Nagot's book was one of a series of similar books published in France in the 18th and early 19th centuries. This genre gained popularity at the time of the revocation of the Edict of Nantes, and came back into vogue in the 19th century because of the reinstatement of the Church after the French Revolution. The popularity of these works is testimony to the fact that generally the French Catholic clergy in Nagot's era were not in favor of religious pluralism. See Michèle Sàcquin, *Entre Bossuet et Maurras: L'Antiprotestantisme en France de 1814 à 1870* (Paris: École des Cartes, 1998), 214.

16 Shortly after Thayer arrived in the U.S., Carroll expressed some concerns about him. See, e.g., Thomas O'Brien Hanley, (ed.), *The Carroll Papers.* I (Notre Dame: University of Notre Dame, 1976), 434, 442-443.

17 This is contained in a letter dated September 28, 1790, and published in the second edition of Nagot's work on Thayer entitled, *Recueil de Conversions Remarquables, nouvellement opérées dans quelques protestants* (Paris: Crapart, 1791), 84-128.

François de Martineau (1763-1788), was of assistance to Nagot and Emery during the reform of the *Petit Séminaire*.[18]

Also, as superior of the *Petit Séminaire,* Nagot began writing a biography of Father Olier.[19] The idea for this project came from Emery whose reform of the Seminary, with the help of Nagot, was based on the spirit and writings of Olier.[20] Yet Emery recognized that what had been written up to that time about the life of the founder was inadequate.[21]

Nagot probably worked on this project for several years, and in it he cited Olier's *Mémoires* for the first time. Apparently a text of the biography was ready in 1790,[22] and he and Emery planned to have it published in 1791. However, the events of that fateful year made publication impractical. The work was only published by the Society in 1818, two years after Nagot's death. The work inspired many priests and it also stirred a revival of interest in the thought of Olier himself.[23]

In addition to publishing these three works, Nagot expressed his zeal for priestly formation by creating new programs. He was very concerned about the quality of the education that his seminarians were receiving prior to entering the

---

18 See Gosselin, I, 185. In other words, Thayer's fervor seemed to match that of Nagot and served as a catalyst for reform in the community.

19 See Ch. I, n. 5, above. We do not know for sure just when this work was begun. Gosselin wrote that a text was ready at the end of 1788. See Gosselin, I, 194. Bertrand noted that the earliest existing manuscript is dated in 1790. The Sulpician historian Father Faillon wrote in 1841 only that Nagot's work, then out-of-print and unavailable, was composed *"peu de temps avant la révolution."* The success of this work motivated Faillon to write a new, more complete and more influential biography. See Faillon, *Vie,* 1ˢᵗ ed., I, xxix-xxx. Nagot's biography is not a scholarly one by today's standards. It is more of an appreciation on Olier's life and spirituality.

20 Gosselin, I, 193-194. *"M. Emery n'ignorait pas qu'il était l'héritier de la pensée de M. Olier; qu'il ne pouvait sans une trahison sacrilège en faire l'abandon, et qu'il devait,* à *l'exemple de son maître, travailler de toutes ses forces et d'une manière exclusive à cette œuvre, assez grande pour répondre à son ambition chrétienne et à son activité, faire des prêtres selon le cœur de Jésus-Christ."* See Élie Méric, *Histoire de M. Emery et de l'Eglise de France pendant la Révolution,* I (Paris: Poussielgue, 1895), 81. By turning to Olier, Emery moved beyond Tronson.

21 Father Gilles Chaillot, P.S.S., has written that the memory of Olier himself had almost been lost in the 18ᵗʰ century. See Molac, 301.

22 Bertrand, II, 43

23 Ibid. and see Faillon, *Vie,* 1ˢᵗ ed., I, xxix-xxx. See also The Minutes of the General Council Meeting of January 28, 1817 (Paris: a bound handwritten collection of minutes in the SAP), 529. There it says that *"ancien évêque"* Bausset had read Nagot's biography of Olier and recommended its publication. This must have been Louis-François de Bausset (1748-1824), retired bishop of Alés and a well-known writer and educator, who was named a cardinal in 1817. He was an alumnus of Saint Sulpice in Paris and was close to Emery.

Seminary.[24] This concern was caused by two factors.[25] First, after the suppression of the Jesuits, education on the secondary level was no longer of the quality and kind that Nagot himself had received.[26] Second, as France approached the era of the Revolution, the number of those entering the seminary was declining due to increasing religious indifference in the educational system.[27] So Nagot decided to do something about this by developing two new pre-seminary programs, like minor seminaries elsewhere.[28]

The first of these, called the Community for Young Clerics, was started in 1786.[29] The program served 25-30 students in their late teens who lived in a house on the rue Cassette, near the Seminary. For their academic work, these student attended local colleges but they had their religious instruction at their residence where there was also a spiritual formation program modeled on the one at the *Petit Séminaire*. In establishing this program, Nagot was assisted by the Sulpician Jean-Joseph de Tersac (1739-1788),[30] then the pastor of Saint Sulpice, and especially by Abbé Armand-Louis Le Juge de Bouzonville (1746-1830),[31] a non-Sulpician priest-aristocrat who provided the money needed to purchase the building. Probably at Nagot's recommendation, Father Emery appointed the young Sulpician Jean-François de Savine as the first superior of this new pre-seminary program.[32]

---

24 Melville, 23, put it this way, "Greatly disturbed by the irreligious education of French youth on the eve of the Revolution, the seminary head believed that one solution lay in opening boarding schools firmly based on religious principles."

25 Gosselin, I, 189. See also Joseph-Maxence Péronne, *Vie de Monseigneur de Simony: évêque de Soissons et Laon* (Paris: Louis Vivès, 1861), 27. "*Le zèle de M. Nagot était infatigable et semblait croître avec les dangers qui menaçaient l'Église….La pensée qui le préoccupait surtout était l'éducation chrétienne de l'enfance. Les doctrines irréligieuses et impies, semées à plaisir depuis un demi-siècle dans toute la France, s'insinuaient jusqu'au sein des familles chrétiennes, et menaçaient d'y corrompre dans les enfants, jusqu'aux germes de la société.* [The zeal of Father Nagot was untiring and seemed to grow with the dangers that threatened the Church….What worried him in a special way was the Christian education of the young. The irreligious and irreverent teachings, spread with delight during a half century in all of France, insinuated themselves even into the heart of Christian families, and from there threatened to mislead the children, even to the sources of society.] "

26 Some philosophes and others thought that the Jesuit colleges had been too traditional and overly committed to the priorities of an older and less utilitarian humanism, e.g., the Jesuits overstressed the knowledge of classical languages. The 1860's secular critique of Jesuit education in France is summarized in Natasha Gill, *Educational Philosophy in the French Enlightenment: From Nature to Second Nature* (Surrey: Ashgate, 2010), 69ff. See also Chapter 1 of W. D. Halls, *Education, Culture and Politics in Modern France* (Oxford: Pergamon, 1976). See also Raymond A. Schroth, *The American Jesuits: A History* (New York: New York University, 2007), 50.

27 Tackett, 338-341.

28 Up to this time, the Sulpicians in Paris had focused on the training of older students.

29 Le R. P. Hélyot, *Dictionnaire des ordres religieux*, III, in L'Abbe Migne, *Encyclopédie théologique*, XXI (Paris: Ateliers Catholique de Petit-Montrouge, 1850), Cols. 589-590. See also Gosselin, II, 189-190.

30 Father Tersac was Voltaire's pastor during his final year (Voltaire's funeral was held at Saint Sulpice in 1778), and he was also responsible for the organ of Saint Sulpice, dedicated in 1781.

31 Bouzonville fled to Germany during the Revolution where he continued to serve as spiritual director of Louise Adélaïde de Bourbon-Condé, daughter of the prince of Condé and an abbess. After the Revolution, he was named a canon of Saint-Denis and the vicar general of Nancy.

32 Father de Savine (along with the superiors of the *Robertins* and of *les Philosophes*) was martyred at the Carmes in 1792 and later beatified.

Encouraged by the success of this program on the rue Cassette, in 1788 Nagot began to think about how to improve the education of even younger students and encourage their interest in priesthood. So, in the spring of 1790, he invited the brilliant and newly ordained DuBourg, not yet a Sulpician, to open a school in Issy-les-Moulineaux, a suburb of Paris, to help prepare boys in their early teens for eventual entry into the seminary. Fr. Emery gave unenthusiastic approval to this new program because by that time he was concerned about the survival of the existing Sulpician houses everywhere in France.[33]

BISHOP SIMONY

Nagot had DuBourg rent a property at 20 rue de Noyers in Issy that came to be known as "Monsieur DuBourg's House." Nagot saw that he was assisted there by six seminarians, "most of whom were not yet tonsured."[34] His senior assistant was 20-year-old Abbé Jules-François de Simony (1770-1849), a penitent/directee of Nagot and also a future bishop.[35] The school would be in operation for only about two years because the French Revolution forced DuBourg and the others to flee in order to avoid arrest.[36]

Though Nagot's energy was primarily focused on the formation of seminarians,[37] he also ministered to others who lived outside the seminary.

---

33 It is also sometimes said that Emery had reservations about the young DuBourg. Melville tells us that Emery thought DuBourg to have "an ardent enormous imagination" but that he also tended to discount the downside of what he envisioned. So, though he was talented, Emery thought him as somewhat impetuous. Nevertheless, Emery added, "If it *is* [sic] a defect, it is preferable to pusillanimity." See Melville, 18-19.

34 Ibid., 24.

35 Pérrone, 25. Simony was bishop of Soisson from 1825-1847.

36 In the late summer of 1792, DuBourg, 26 and not yet a Sulpician, fled to Bordeaux and then to Spain where many Sulpicians and thousands of other French priests lived as unwelcome exiles. In 1793 France went to war against Spain, making their exile more difficult. In 1795 DuBourg sailed to the U.S. to join Nagot. More on this later. See Melville, 30ff.

37 The Sulpician Constitutions at the time did not encourage Sulpicians to take on significant responsibilities outside the seminary. See Henri d'Antin de Vaillac, *Les constitutions de la compagnie de Saint-Sulpice, Etude historique et canonique* (Paris: unpublished doctoral thesis at the Institut Catholique, 1965), I, 49, and II, 215-216. Moreover, just as today, superiors like Nagot had more than enough to do in running their seminary programs.

First, he worked toward the conversion of some young Protestants.[38] One of them may have been an Englishman named Francis Tulloch whom we will meet later. Another was Alexander Dick (1763-1823) from Edinburgh. Once an indifferent Scottish Presbyterian, Dick was admitted into the Church in 1795 by the prominent apologist Bishop George Hay (1729-1811).[39] Decades later Dick published a book about his conversion. In it he wrote about his visit to the Sulpician Seminary in Paris in 1787. During that visit, he read Thayer's story of conversion and then met Thayer himself. He also discussed religion with Nagot and learned from him about the conversion of another protestant. Here is Dick's glowing description of Nagot:

> The other [Catholic priest who influenced me] was M. Nagot, one of the superiors of Saint Sulpice, a venerable old man, whose gray hairs commanded respect, and whose serene and smiling countenance inspired affection and regard. Filled with the most fervent and genuine devotion, it could not be confined to his heart alone, but appeared in all his exterior; and though he spoke his sentiments with great freedom and plainness, his conversation, so far from being any way stiff and repulsive, was, like his whole deportment, simple, natural and singularly attractive.[40]

---

38 [Garnier?], 287. We are not sure who all of these converts were. One may have been John Caldwell. More below.

39 See Anonymous, "Shorter Notices," *The Rambler*, I, no. 7 (Feb. 12, 1848), 124. More on Hay below.

40 This citation can be found in its entirety in a review of Dick's work in Charles Dolman, *Dolman's Magazine and Monthly Miscellany of Criticism*, 1848, 378.

Dick also left us a copy of an important letter that Nagot wrote to him on Dec. 13, 1788, shortly after his visit to Paris. In it, Nagot urged Dick to convert to the Catholic faith in these words:

> I cannot conceal from you that I still have hopes of seeing you with us. And on what are my hopes founded? On the infinite goodness of the heart of Jesus who, in spite of the ingratitude of yours, still seeks you, and calls upon you to surrender to Him; – on the happy inconsistencies which I remark [sic] in your own heart, for in spite of all its endeavors to make you regard the Catholic religion as an illusion, it contradicts itself by making you feel so much sweetness in that illusion, and so much pleasure in recollecting the time you passed amongst Catholics…What then shall I say to you? That I shall not cease to pray for you and to love you.[41]

Adding to the impact of this letter, Nagot noted that he was writing it from the bedside of the dying seminarian-convert Martineau, mentioned earlier, whom Dick had also met in Paris. In the published account of his conversion, Dick explained that Nagot's letter remained in the back of his mind and, five years later, helped to lead him into the Church.[42]

To understand fully the significance of Nagot's efforts to bring Dick and others like him into the Church, it is helpful to know that, during the 18th century, the Holy See considered England, Scotland and Wales to be mission territories. The main reason was that, after centuries of draconian penal legislation against Catholics, the vast majority of people in those regions were no longer Catholic. For example, it was estimated that in 1780 there were less than 60,000 Catholics in England and Wales out of a total population of about six million,[43] and there was continuing pressure on Catholics to leave the Church.[44]

Along with the status of missions, England, Scotland and Wales did not have

---

41 A Convert [Alexander Dick], *Reasons for Embracing the Catholic Faith* (Edinburgh: James Marshal; and London: Dolman, Jones, and Burns, 1848), 42-43.

42 Ibid., 57-58.

43 See Basil Hemphill, *The Early Vicars Apostolic of England, 1685-1750* (London: Burns & Oates, 1954), 102. A more recent estimate is 70,000. See Hubert Jedin (ed.), *History of the Church*, VI (New York: Crossroad, 1981), 177.

44 These law were lifted during the brief reign of James II, when there were still about 300,000 professed Catholics. Ibid. However, the Glorious Revolution in 1688 reinstated these laws. See, e.g., Chapter VI of Hemphill. In Scotland, the insurrection of 1745 in favor of Bonnie Prince Charlie (i.e., Charles Stuart, or The Young Pretender, 1720-1788) led to stricter enforcement of penal laws against Catholics there. Those who supported the Stuart claims were called Jacobites (a reference to James II).

diocesan bishops during that period. In fact, except for about a decade during the reign of the ill-fated Charles I (1600-1649), there had been no diocesan bishops in those territories since Queen Mary I (i.e., Mary Tudor, 1516-1558) briefly restored the hierarchy in the mid-16th century. So, in Nagot's time, the Church there was led by vicars apostolic, under the authority of the Congregation for the Propagation of the Faith in Rome.[45] That is why Bishop George Hay, who received Dick into the Church, had the title of vicar apostolic of the Scottish Lowlands.[46]

These vicars apostolic had a very difficult ministry. They tried both to sustain the faith of the few Catholics that remained loyal and to encourage the reconversion of the population to Catholicism when possible. A serious obstacle to the latter task was legal: the evangelization of non-Catholics was a crime with severe penalties.[47]

Starting in 1788, however, the British Parliament, under George III, began to pass "relief acts" for Catholics, acts that did not repeal the penal laws but lessened their sting. The first one, called The Papists Act, caused an anti-Catholic

THE GORDON RIOTS

---

45 This is the arrangement in some mission territories today. The original appointment of these vicars apostolic in England and Wales was one of the only lasting contributions of James II.

46 Scotland, where there was stronger sympathy for the Catholic Stuarts, only got vicars apostolic in 1731.

47 Ibid., 87. At the beginning of the 18th century, the death penalty was replaced by life in prison. Jedin, 177.

riot in London, called the Gordon Riots.[48] This was followed by another relief act in 1791. These acts eventually led to the repeal of the penal laws against Catholics in 1829. They also created an environment in which it was easier for non-Catholics like Dick to return to the Old Faith, and the number of conversions increased significantly during the period of the relief acts. In light of these developments at the end of the 18th century, Nagot's effort to convert Dick and others like him was a contribution to missionary work in Britain, but done from the safety of Paris.

FATHER EDGEWORTH (BNF)

Nagot also helped clerics in France who sought him out. Foremost among these was the famous Abbé Henry Essex Edgeworth de Firmont (1745-1807).[49] Nagot served as his spiritual director/confessor, and Dilhet believed,[50] probably wrongly, that Edgeworth had attended the Sulpician Seminary under Nagot.[51] Edgeworth was the son of an Anglo-Irish minister who had converted to Catholicism when the younger Edgeworth was just a child. In 1749 he and most of his immediate family moved from British Ireland to Toulouse, France, in order to escape the burdens of penal legislation against Catholics.

---

48 This riot was also fueled by France's actions during the American Revolution.

49 See [Garnier?], 287. In a letter from Father Emery to Father Babad, dated January 22, 1793, Emery says that Edgeworth confessed to Nagot before the latter left for America. See Delarc, 9.

50 See Ruane, 162-163, for some deficiencies in Dilhet's recollections.

51 Jean Dilhet, État de l'église catholique ou Diocèse des États-Unis de l'Amérique septentrionale, trans. Patrick Browne (Washington, D.C.: Salve Regina Press, 1922), 172. Edgeworth's obituary tells us, however, that Edgeworth prepared for priesthood at the College of Navarre and at the Sorbonne while living at the Collége des Trente-Trois, a residence for poor students. See Anonymous, Obituary of Henry Essex Edgeworth in The Annual Biography and Obituary for the Year, 4 (London: Longman, Rees, etc., 1820), 448. See also M. V. Woodgate, The Abbé Edgeworth (1745-1807) (Dublin: Browne & Nolan, 1945), 15; and Violette M. Montagu, The Abbe Edgeworth and His Friends (London: Herbert Jenkins, 1913), 7. At the same time, Gosselin, I, 335-336, tells us that Edgeworth had a long association with the Sulpician Seminary, and we know from one of Edgeworth's letters that an acquaintance named Jasper studied at Saint Sulpice. When Jasper decided to go there, Edgeworth was concerned at first: the seminary was full of worldly and ambitious aristocrats. However, Edgeworth wrote that he looked into the matter and learned, "It is still one of the best seminaries in Paris." See Henry Essex Edgeworth de Firmont, Letters from the Abbe Edgeworth to His Friends, Written between the Years of 1777 and 1807 (London: Longman, Hurst, etc., 1818), 29.

After being ordained in Paris, Edgeworth earned a reputation as an excellent priest. In a tribute to him, it was said,

> Never did man shew [sic] more invariable benignity and gentleness or a piety more consoling to his fellow creatures. This evangelical man was often seen with a countenance radiant with joy, surrounded by the poor, and the lower orders of workingmen in Paris, leading them to his tribunal of peace.[52]

Because of this reputation, according to a close relative, Edgeworth was offered a diocese in Ireland, but he declined, with the support of his confessor.[53] Unfortunately, by his middle age, poor health forced Edgeworth to cut back on his ministerial commitments.

Edgeworth became famous during the French Revolution. In 1791, at the age of 46, he was asked to become the confessor of a princess known as Madame Élisabeth of France (1764-1794), sister of Louis XVI.[54] Late that same year, through her influence, he also became the confessor of the King himself. As

EDGEWORTH AT THE EXECUTION OF LOUIS XVI

---

52 Edgeworth, C. S, ed. *Memoirs of the Abbé Edgeworth, Containing His Narrative of the Last Hours of Louis XVI.* (London, Rowland Hunter, 1815), 10-11.

53 Ibid., 12. His confessor at that time may have been Nagot. Also one biographer of Edgeworth says that he was offered more than one diocese in Ireland but turned them all down. See Woodgate, 23.

54 Ibid., 14. He remained faithful to her until her execution in 1794.

such, he accompanied the King to his execution in 1793[55] and left to posterity a memorable account of that event.[56]

Another notable outsider that Father Nagot counseled was a princess known as Madame Louise of France (1737-1787), the youngest daughter of King Louis

XV and the aunt of King Louis XVI. Raised by a governess at the Abbey of Fontevrault, Louise felt a call to religious life early on. However, her father was more interested in finding a useful marriage partner for her. Nevertheless, in 1770 he relented and let her enter the strict Carmel of Saint Denis where she took the name Thérèse de Saint-Augustin.[57]

She became known "for her ardent love of God," and in 1773 she was elected prioress.[58] During the reign of her nephew Louis XVI, she encouraged and prayed for him and for his wife. However, in 1787 she died very suddenly, probably as a result

MOTHER THÉRÈSE DE SAINT-AUGUSTIN

of poisoning by a radical anti-monarchist. We know only that she asked for Nagot's advice, that he visited her at times, and that she suffered great spiritual trials toward the end of her life.[59]

Any account of Nagot's time as superior of the *Petit Séminaire* would not be complete without noting that he had the dubious honor of serving as spiritual director/confessor of the young aristocrat Charles-Maurice de Talleyrand-

---

55 Coincidentally, James Ussher, the 17th century Protestant archbishop of Armagh and a relative of Edgeworth, attended the execution of Charles I in 1649.

56 Ibid. Early in the Revolution, the archbishop of Paris fled the country and in 1791, he appointed Edgeworth as a *grand vicaire*. Emery was also a *grand vicaire* of Paris, and in 1795, during Emery's imprisonments, he was put on trial for conspiring with Edgeworth who was considered a counter-revolutionary. See Gosselin, I, 335ff. Edgeworth himself managed to evade capture during the Terror by staying underground and moving often. In 1807 Edgeworth died from disease in the Russian city of Mittau, now in Latvia, while ministering to Louis XVIII and the royal family in exile.

57 Thayer, who called her Madame Louisa, considered her heroic example to be a testimony to the truth of Catholicism. Thayer, 35.

58 See Raymond Arricau, "Teresa of St. Augustine (Louise of France, 1737-1787)" at http://carmelnet.org/biographies/TeresaStAugustine.pdf (accessed 10/1/15). She was declared "venerable" in 1873.

59 Ibid. See also [Garnier?], 287

Périgord who appeared earlier in this text[60] and who will reappear later on. The oldest son of Count Charles-Daniel de Talleyrand-Périgord, Charles-Maurice was baptized at the parish of Saint Sulpice. Due to a deformity of his foot, he was blocked from inheriting his father's title because the younger Talleyrand was not able to pursue the traditional military career of the counts of Périgord.

CARDINAL ALEXANDRE TALLEYRAND

As a result, though he had limited enthusiasm for it, he agreed to take up an ecclesiastical career and he was a seminarian at the *Grand Séminaire* for a time in the early to mid-1770s. Oral tradition has it that the Sulpicians, including Nagot, did not think that he had a vocation, and they discouraged him from pursuing ordination. In support of this tradition, it can be said that he did not receive Holy Orders while at the Seminary.[61] He only completed his licentiate at the Sorbonne in 1778[62] and was ordained a priest in 1779.

His father was close to the king and, of course, strongly promoted his ecclesiastical career. His uncle, Alexandre-Angélique de Talleyrand-Périgord (1736-1821), was coadjutor archbishop of Reims when Charles-Maurice was a seminarian, and became the ordinary in 1777. So he too was in an excellent position to aid his flawed nephew. Immediately upon his ordination as a priest, Charles-Maurice was appointed *grand vicaire* of Reims, and in 1788 he became bishop of Autun at the age of 34. In 1790 he would be one out of only six French bishops (out of eighty-three) who took the oath of loyalty to The Civil Consitution of the Clergy.[63] In January 1791, he would ordain bishops without papal approval and so he was intimately involved in the creation of the schismatic Constitutional Church.[64] More on this later.

60 See page 20, above. Evidence of Nagot's relationship with Talleyrand can be found in notes entitled, "Conversation avec M. Castelnau Père ancien Éleve de la communauté de Laon," Matériaux , XII, 154. These notes are at the end of the volume.

61 Gosselin, I, 257.

62 This degree was a prerequisite for appointment as a *grand vicaire*.

63 See Tackett, 545.

64 At the Nuncio's request, Emery sent three seminarians to this consecration to get information about it. Afterwards, Emery exclaimed, "*Voilà un grand scandale!*" Gosselin, I, 257.

In 1791 Talleyrand resigned the episcopacy in order to go into politics, an occupation for which he was better suited. After surviving the Terror by fleeing to the U.S. for two years,[65] he became foreign minister of France. Napoleon I gave him a great title, something he had always wanted, appointing him Prince of Benevento in 1806. After the fall of Napoleon, Talleyrand promoted the restoration of the monarchy and represented France at the Congress of Vienna. He is considered one of history's ablest diplomats. The fact that he had a lax conscience did not seem to impede his success in this arena.

That the young Talleyrand picked Nagot as his confessor/director showed good judgment on his part. Nevertheless, little of Nagot's piety seems to have rubbed off on him, and Nagot certainly does not deserve credit for Talleyrand's darker exploits.[66]

PRINCE TALLEYRAND

---

65 We will see that he met Nagot there.

66 Talleyrand later developed a reputation for being both sensual and venal. One of his many critics, the Comte de Mirabeau, once said that Talleyrand would ""sell his soul for money and he would be right for he would be exchanging dung for gold."" See François Furstenburg, *When America Spoke French: Five Refugees Who Shaped a Nation* (New York: Penguin Books, 2015), 8.

VI

MINISTRY AT THE GRAND SÉMINAIRE
(1789-1791)

During his final two years in Paris, Father Nagot was given even more responsibility. First, the regular General Assembly of May 7-23, 1789 elected him an assistant of the Society and then as the first alternate for membership on the general council.[1] To understand what these elections meant, it is necessary to know something about the Society's internal structure at the time.[2] The Constitutions inherited from Father Olier's successor Father Alexandre Le Ragois de Bretonvilliers (1621-1676), and further expanded in 1717, specified that the leadership of the community was in the hands of the superior general and twelve assistants. Together they constituted a body called the general assembly of the Society which ordinarily met every six years. It was this body that set policy for the Society and elected the superior general and their own membership by majority votes. These leaders had unlimited terms of office.

From among the assistants, the assembly also elected four regular consultors to work more closely with the superior general and two substitute, or alternate, consultors. These substitute consultors were required to take the place of one or more regular consultors if they were not able to attend a scheduled meeting.[3] So, Nagot's election as one of the twelve assistants and as the first alternate consultor gave him special responsibility for the mission and welfare of the entire Society.

FATHER BRETONVILLIERS

It is also relevant to know that, according to the Constitutions of the Society then in force, those qualified to be assistants were to have "an abundance of the Apostolic Spirit" and should have demonstrated for some time "the chief signs

---

1 Nagot was elected as an assistant during the fourth session, on May 18. See the Minutes of the General Assemblies of the Society of Saint Sulpice, III (Paris: bound handwritten document in the SAP, n.d.), 105. He was elected first alternate consultor during the tenth session, on May 23. See ibid., 117. Nagot did not begin to sign the daily copies of minutes until the 9th session, but the minutes of May 21 indicate that Nagot was absent because of his duties at the seminary. See ibid., 116.

2 For the basis of this description, see Gosselin, I, 5ff.

3 Vaillac explained that a quorum consisted of the general and four consultors, regular or substitute. See Vaillac, I, 82.

of virtue."[4] Thus Nagot would have been a natural choice to be an assistant.

Second, it is not surprising that in that same year, Nagot, at 55, was transferred by Emery to the *Grand Séminaire* where he would serve as "*supérieur second*," or vice-rector in today's parlance.[5] At that time, there were eleven on the formation team, including Emery and Nagot.[6] Since Emery was also serving as superior general, Nagot had much responsibility for running that program on a day-to-day basis.[7] So this transfer is also testimony to Emery's trust in and esteem for him at that time.

While at the *Grand Séminaire*, Nagot apparently served as spiritual director/confessor of a young seminarian named Guillaume-Aubin de Villèle (1770-

1841).[8] He came from a prominent royalist family, and after the Revolution, his cousin Jean-Baptiste-Joseph, count of Villèle (1773-1854), served as premier of France under Kings Louis XVIII and Charles X. Guillaume-Aubin himself would later become a highly revered bishop, first of Verdun and then of Soisson. In 1824 he would be named archbishop of Bourges, and he is considered the architect of the restoration of that archdiocese.[9] We will

VILLÈLE FAMILY ARMS   encounter him again.

Finally, while at the *Grand Séminaire*, Nagot also got to know a young man named Jean-Edouard de Mondésir (1770-1844) who was a seminarian of the Diocese of Chartres and was enrolled in the *Robertins*. Nagot served as his confessor/director.[10] Mondésir admired Nagot because of his prayerfulness and would agree to accompany him to the U.S. We will hear much more from Mondésir below.

---

4 "*...avoir en plénitude l'Esprit Apostolique et avoir durant plusieurs années...de grandes marques de vertu.*" Ibid., 81.

5 In a list of non-juring Sulpicians at the *Grand Séminaire,* both Bossard and Delarc gave this title to Nagot. See Clément Bossard, *Histoire du serment à Paris* (Paris, chez tous les marchands des nouveautés, 1791), 75. See also Odon Delarc, *L'église de Paris pendant la révolution française, 1789-1801*, I (Paris: Desclée, de Brouwer, 1895), 372. Gosselin, 96, called him the "*premier directeur.*" See also Vaillac, I, 80, where he explains that the Constitutions spoke of the special assistance given to the superior general by "*le Directeur du Séminaire.*" This probably explains Mondésir's cryptic reference to Nagot's position on page 75, below.

6 Bossard, 75, and Delarc, 372.

7 See, e.g., note 5, above.

8 Villèle was very well known to the Sulpicians since he had studied under them for many years in Paris, probably at the Community for Young Clerics that was founded by Nagot, and afterwards at the Sulpician Seminary itself. He corresponded with Nagot after Nagot arrived in the U.S. and the tone of this correspondence implies that Nagot was his director. Villèle was also close to Emery, and they too corresponded during the Revolution. For a biography of Villèle, see M. S. Boullée, "de Villèle," *Biographies contemporaines,* I (Paris: Auguste Vaton, 1863), 229-233.

9 See Guy Devailly, *Le Diocèse de Bourges.* (Paris: Letouzey & Ané, 1973), 177.

10 See *Matériaux* , IV, 511.

VII

VISIT TO ENGLAND

In 1789 dramatic political events exacerbated Father Emery's already deep concern about the future of his community in France and eventually led to Father Nagot's departure from that country.[1] First, because Louis XVI had failed to find a way to bolster the image of the monarchy and solve France's economic problems, in July of 1788 he was forced to convoke a meeting of the Estates General, the first such meeting in more than 150 years. The Estates General consisted of representatives of the three "orders" of the realm, namely the clergy (the First Estate), the nobility (the Second Estate), and the common people (the Third Estate).[2] However, on June 17, 1789, the representatives of the common people withdrew from the Estates General and declared themselves to be a National Assembly, the true embodiment of the will of the people of France.[3]

Second, less than a month later, a mob in Paris stormed the Bastille, the hated prison for those who were deemed disloyal to the monarchy. This event is seen as the beginning of the French Revolution, and in August, 1789, the attention of the National Assembly would shift towards a sweeping overhaul of the Church in France.[4]

CARTOON OF THE THREE ESTATES

---

1 After the French and Indian War, many French Sulpicians in Canada returned to France, and the British government would not allow additional French Sulpicians to settle in Montreal. See Molac, 72-73.

2 Up to then, even though they represented the vast majority of the French population, the Third Estate was dominated by the two privileged groups, the First Estate and the Second Estate. The main method of domination consisted in the fact that when issues were decided at meetings of the Estates General, the votes of each of the two privileged Estates were deemed equal to that of the First Estate.

3 The National Assembly morphed into the National Constituent Assembly in July 1789 and then established the Legislative Assembly in September 1791. In this work, to avoid unnecessary confusion, the term National Assembly will be used to refer to all three of these bodies that ruled during the first three years of the French Revolution.

4 For more detail, see Tackett, 541ff.

STORMING OF THE BASTILLE

Finally, a month before the storming of the Bastille, the danger was driven home to Father Emery when he was informed that a mob was gathering and intended to ransack the house of the Vincentians, called Saint-Lazare, and the Sulpician Seminary. Emery quickly devised measures to placate it, if possible, but fortunately he did not have to use those measures because the pillage of the Vincentian house seemed to exhaust the mob's rage.

By this time, on the other side of the Atlantic, conditions were improving for Catholics. In 1783, the Treaty of Paris recognized the political independence of the United States and added greatly to its territory. The next year the Holy See gave the Church in the U.S. canonical independence by appointing the former Jesuit Father John Carroll (1735-1815) as prefect apostolic of the new nation, reporting directly to the Holy See.

During the American Revolution, some of the states had already disestablished the Church of England. Maryland did so in 1776. The new Constitution of the U.S., approved by Congress in 1787, did not create an established national church but allowed for religious freedom. This was something that had been denied to Catholics in the British colonies since the "Glorious Revolution" one hundred years earlier. The new Constitution went into effect in 1788, and on

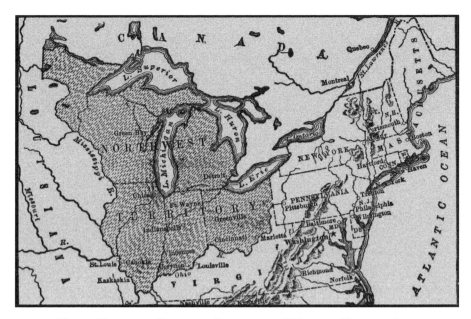

MAP OF NORTHWEST TERRITORY, CEDED TO THE U.S. BY THE TREATY OF PAIRS

April 30, 1789, George Washington was inaugurated as the first president.

In light of these encouraging developments, the Holy See agreed to establish a hierarchy in the United States. So in May of 1789 the clergy of the U.S. met at Whitemarsh, Maryland, and proposed their Prefect Apostolic John Carroll, 54, for appointment as the first bishop. He was appointed as bishop of Baltimore on November 6 of that year.

As prefect apostolic, he had reported to the authorities in Rome that he had only a few priests, some of them quite old, to serve his faithful who were spread over a vast territory.[5] He also expressed his hope that the development of Catholic colleges in the U.S. would lead to more native

BISHOP CARROLL

---

5 See Hanley, I, 181. Carroll chose an appropriate motto for his difficult ministry: *"Ne derelinquas nos Domine Deus Noster,"* i.e., "Forsake us not, O Lord Our God."

vocations.[6] Accordingly, in his bull of appointment, he was commissioned, among other things, "to establish an episcopal seminary."[7] Yet in 1790 he had a total of only 34 priests, about half of whom were former Jesuits.[8]

Meanwhile, back in Paris, with the skies darkening over France, Father Emery was making plans to preserve his community and its ministry. According to Sulpician Jean Dilhet (1753-1811), Father Gaspard de Saint Félix (1741-1832), the Sulpician superior in Toulouse, suggested to Emery that he consider starting a Sulpician mission overseas.[9] Then Father Jacques-Gabriel Gallais (1754-1792), a Sulpician who was superior of the *Robertins*, made a concrete suggestion.[10] He knew that some French families with royalist sympathies were moving to the U.S. and settling on the banks of the Ohio River, not far from the western border of Virginia.[11] So he recommended to Emery that he send some Sulpicians to minister to those émigrés. Emery may also have had the idea of sending some Sulpicians even further west to minister to other small French-speaking settlements on the Wabash River in present-day Indiana or on the Mississippi River in present-day southern Illinois.[12]

---

6 Ibid., 174. This was an important part of Carroll's thinking in relation to Georgetown. See John Daley, *Georgetown University: Origin and Early Years* (Washington, DC: Georgetown University, 1957), Ch. II.

7 Peter Guilday, *The Life and Times of John Carroll* (New York: The Encyclopedia Press, 1922), 360. Guilday gives an English translation of the entire document.

8 John R. Dichtl, *Frontiers of Faith: Bringing Catholicism to the West in the Early Republic.* (Lexington, KY: University Press of Kentucky, 2008), 22.

9 Dilhet, 15. Dilhet worked with Father Nagot in the summer and fall of 1806 and may have received this information from him.

10 In 1792 Father Gallais was martyred at the Carmes and was later beatified.

11 Their settlement was called Gallipolis, or City of the Gauls, and today it is a town in southeastern Ohio. However, in the late 1780's, there was no Ohio or West Virginia, and everything north and west of the Ohio River was part of what would be called the Northwest Territory. See John McGovern, "The Gallipolis Colony in Ohio: 1786-1793," *Records of the American Catholic Historical Society*, XXXVII (1926), 26-72. See also Dilhet, 172-174.

12 Ibid. Although Kauffman, following Ruane, leaves the reader with the impression that the missionary effort was entirely Carroll's initiative, it is clear that providing ministers for remote French-speaking settlements was part of Emery's original plan. See Kauffman, 39-41. See also Pierre Rousseau, *Saint-Sulpice et les mission catholiques* (Montreal: Edouard Garand, 1930), 168-169. See also Méric, 124-125. For Emery's thinking, see the transcript of Emery's letter to Carroll of August 25, 1790 in I, 32. In Carroll's reply to Emery, dated September 3, 1790, Carroll discussed some concrete options in a part of the letter not found in Hanley, probably because the archived draft of Carroll's letter is far from the finished product. However, a transcription of the missing portion can be found in Anonymous, "Eglise Catholique du Maryland," *Annales de la religion et du sentiment, Seconde Ann*é (1792), No. VI, 143ff. See Gabrielle Guillerm, *La Contribution française aux débuts de l' Église catholique des Etats-Unis (1790-1850)*, (Paris: unpublished master's thesis at the Université Paris Sorbonne, 2013), 135. A copy of this work is available at the SAP, Paris. Sulpician missionaries from Quebec knew about and visited these settlements long before the time of Emery and Carroll.

As he pondered these possibilities, Emery wisely consulted with the Nuncio in Paris, Archbishop, later Cardinal, Antonio Dugnani (1748-1818) who was informed about the needs of the Church in the U.S.[13] Dugnani told him about the impending consecration of John Carroll and about his need for a seminary.

Then Emery called an extraordinary general assembly of the Society to discuss some very pressing matters.[14] Nagot attended this assembly, which was held from August 12-15, 1790. It turned out to be his last assembly – because of the Revolution, the next one was not held until 1802.

The second topic on the agenda was whether the Society should take this opportunity to send men to America. This issue, so important for Nagot's future, was taken up on August 12 in the second session of the assembly. At the beginning of the session, Emery shared what he had learned from the

CARDINAL DUGNANI

Nuncio and asked for a discussion. The assembly then addressed the advantages of taking such an initiative, including the belief that since Father Olier had assisted in Canada, the Society would only reaffirm its historic identity if it were to assist a distant local church in need.[15] Of course, it was also noted that this initiative would provide a place of refuge for French Sulpicians and a place where the Society could continue its ministry. The Assembly endorsed the initiative and authorized Emery and the consultors to move forward with it.

So, on August 25 Emery wrote to Carroll, now awaiting his episcopal consecration in England, about the interest of some of his confreres in sending missionaries to French-speaking settlements.[16] He also wrote, "He [Dugnani] thinks, as do I, that it would be much more interesting to set up a seminary in your new diocese, where one might raise up apostolic workers who would

13 Dugnani's predecessor had developed an unsuccessful plan to put the U.S. Church under the authority of a French bishop, and Dugnani and Carroll had corresponded prior to this time.

14 For this discussion, see Minutes of the General Assemblies, III, 120ff.

15 This appeal to Olier would have been powerful in an era when interest in Olier himself was being revived. Also in the 18th century "Canada" was not the name of a country. Rather it was a word from the Huron-Iroquois language that meant a collection of lodges. It was first used in a European document by Jacques Cartier in 1535, and he apparently thought that it was the name of a vast Native American territory.

16 The lack of priests to minister to these settlements had been a concern to Carroll since 1783 when they were separated from Quebec. See Hanley, I, 753. So both Carroll and Emery had an interest in this matter.

ARCHBISHOP CARROLL'S COAT OF ARMS

suffice for the immense harvest which is offered by the United States."[17] Emery then invited Carroll to discuss these ideas with him further either by coming to Paris or, if that was not possible, by receiving his representative in England.[18] Dugnani also wrote to Carroll about his discussion with Emery.

At first, Carroll was somewhat hesitant about the foundation of a seminary so soon because, as he confided to his friend Father Charles Plowden on September 2, he did not have any students who were prepared to enter a major seminary program.[19] Yet the next day he wrote to Emery that, despite this concern, he was open to further dialogue, and he welcomed Emery's offer to send a representative to see him in England.

---

17 "*Il croit, ainsi que moi, qu'il serait bien plus interessant de former un Séminaire, dans votre nouveau Diocèse, ou l'on élevât des ouvriers apostoliques qui puissant suffire à la moisson immense qu'offrent les états unis.*" See Faillon, *Histoire,* I, 32. Kauffman's summary of this meeting seems overly simplistic. See Kauffman, 38. As we shall see, Emery did not abandon his interest in missionary work even though Gallipolis would not be its focus.

18 A transcription of this letter is contained in Faillon, *Histoire*, I, 29-30. See also Hanley, I, 457.

19 Hanley, I, 454.

Emery chose his trusted colleague Nagot to meet with Carroll and to be the leader of the new enterprise. Nagot had proven himself over many years to be a priest with both a deep spirituality and a strong apostolic spirit who was a very effective Sulpician leader. However, if Dilhet's account is accurate,[20] Emery might have sent Saint Félix because Nagot recommended him for the job.[21] However, Dilhet reported that Saint Félix declined, and Emery naturally returned to Nagot. So, in September Nagot set out for London.[22]

He and Carroll were about the same age, and Nagot clearly made a very good impression on Carroll who described him shortly afterwards as a "'worthy and learned priest.'"[23] More to the point, Nagot seems to have overcome Carroll's initial hesitation because, shortly after the visit, Carroll expressed real enthusiasm about the coming of the Sulpicians to Baltimore, characterizing it several times as a sign of divine favor.[24] Of course, given Carroll's meager resources, he was also encouraged by the Sulpicians' willingness to pay for the voyage, to bring some seminarians with them, and to purchase and furnish a facility for the new seminary.[25] In any event, as one noted historian of the Church in America once remarked, "There are indeed few events in the history of the Church in this country which show more plainly the hand of God."[26]

During the winter following the trip to England, Emery and Nagot prepared for the journey. On the logistical level, Emery, undoubtedly assisted by Nagot,[27] chose appropriate companions and raised some funds that were added to a substantial amount of the Society's own funds.[28] He and Nagot also assembled the items that Nagot would take with them, e.g., books and liturgical furnishings. On a programmatic level, Emery composed an interesting document entitled "Counsels and rules of conduct" ("*Conseils et Regles de Conduit*") for those going to establish the new seminary. He was surely relying on Nagot's leadership when

---

20 According to historians, Dilhet's recollections are sometimes not accurate. See, e.g., Ruane, 162-163.

21 Dilhet, 15. If Nagot did make this recommendation, it may have been a result of his humility and it may have been made when Emery approached him first.

22 There is some lack of certainty on exact dates of this visit. Here we follow Hanley, 462, where, on the basis of Carroll's letters, he puts the visit between the 14th and the 18th of September, 1790.

23 Guilday, 468. These words are from Carroll's letter to Dugnani, dated September 19, 1790. The original text of Carroll's description of Nagot was in French and it seemed a bit stronger: "*un Ecclésiastique aussi instruit et respectable en toutes manières.*" See Hanley, 464.

24 Hanley, 464 and 468. "*M. Nagot était un homme de Dieu: son zèle plein de foi, sa piété douce et humble, son coeur affectueux et sa longue expérience de la direction des séminaires, lui méritèrent la confiance de M. Émery et le recommandèrent à l'estime particulière de Mgr Carroll.*" See Méric, I, 126. 167. At the same time, in his correspondence, Carroll often wrote that it was painful to know that his diocese was receiving a great blessing as a result of so much hardship for the Church in France.

25 Hanley, I, 465-466.

26 Guilday, 466.

27 Though the choice of his companions is usually attributed to Emery, Nagot must have proposed the names since, as we will see, most of them were well known to him.

28 Herbermann, 23.

he wrote paragraph 2: "They [the Directors] will neglect nothing to arrive at an eminent holiness, being persuaded that they will do more good through the holiness of their lives than by their teachings and exhortations."[29]

Also, in light of Nagot's evident zeal for the conversion of Protestants, Emery may have written section 7, at least partly, to temper his enthusiasm in preparation for life in a religiously diverse society:

> Although the Directors must be very careful to avoid mixing in the world and seeking to please it, nevertheless, they will strive, especially in the beginning, when they will not be very busy, to be friendly to the people of the city, by rendering service to their children, by giving them, for example, lessons in mathematics, the French language, etc. They must not hesitate to render the same services to the children of Protestants, avoiding any talk of religion, in order not to offend their parents; they will know very well that the very company of the Priests of the Seminary will dispose the children favorably towards the Catholic religion.[30]

There is one final point about the appointment of Nagot that deserves mention. Dilhet wrote, "Though Mr. Nagot was rather old, his zeal for the salvation of souls impelled him to engage in this noble enterprise."[31] One might think that Dilhet's appraisal of Nagot's age, 57 at the time, was only a typical perception of a younger man about an older one - Dilhet was about 20 years younger than Nagot. However, there is a more objective basis for his remark. It may be surprising to know that the normal life expectancy of males at birth in France in the late 18th century was only about 30.[32] Even when you discount this statistic in light of the very high rate of infant mortality, 57 was far from what it is today. McManners tells us, for example, that in the mid-18th century, the average age of death for a military veteran who received good health care and nutrition was the mid to late 60s.[33] This seems representative of those in the population at large

---

29 Jacques-Andre Emery, "Counsels and rules of conduct for the Priests of Saint Sulpice sent, in April 1791, to establish a Seminary in Baltimore, in the United States," trans. Anonymous, (a typed manuscript in the AA, MD), 1, para. 2. This emphasis is paralleled by a corresponding emphasis on the spiritual life of the seminarians. Vaillac explained that as Father Olier was devising the rules to govern his seminary, he wrote: "'*Le principal de ces régles va à l'avancement du progrès spirituel et intérieur.*'" See Vaillac, I, 50.

30 Emery, "Counsels," para. 7.

31 "*Quoique M. Nagot fut d'un âge assez avancé, son zèle pour le salut des âmes l'engagea à entrer dans cette noble entreprise.*" Dilhet, 16. Recall also the comment of Alexander Dick on page 33, above.

32 This data comes from France's Institut National d'étude Démographique. See Anonymous,

"Life expectancy in France," at https://www.ined.fr/en/everything_about_population/graphs-maps/interpreted-graphs/life-expectancy-france/. (accessed 11/2/2015)

33 McManners, I, 65.

who survived childhood.[34] Another scholar has written that during the *ancien régime*, "a man at 50 is already an old man."[35] So Dilhet's emphasis on Nagot's motivation was both appropriate and instructive, highlighting the intensity of Nagot's apostolic spirit. He may have been rather reserved by temperament and he may have been feeling his age, but his sense of mission filled him with energy and enthusiasm.

In February, just before his departure from Paris, Nagot wrote to Dugnani to let him know about the impending voyage and to give him the names of Nagot's traveling companions.[36]

34 See René Baehrel, "*Stastitique et* démographie historique: *la mortalité sous l'ancien régime,*" in *Annales. Économies, Sociétés, Civilisations,* XII (1957), no. 1, 87.

35 "*Un quinquagénaire est déjà un vieillard.*" See Belisaire, "*La population française sous l'Ancien Régime,*" at http://www.philisto.fr/cours-75-la-population-francaise-sous-l-ancien-regime.html.

36 Finbar Kenneally, *United States Documents in the Propaganda Fide Archives: A Calendar,* 1st Series, I (Washington: Academy of American Franciscan History, 1966), 21.

VOYAGE TO THE UNITED STATES

On April 8, 1791[1] Nagot and his companions boarded the 160-ton brig[2] *Saint-Pierre* at St. Malo for a difficult and long voyage to the United States.[3] In his entourage were ten others.

A BRIG LARGER THAN THE *SAINT-PIERRE*

First, there were three younger Sulpicians

- Antoine Garnier (1762-1845), 29, recently a seminarian at the *Robertins*;[4]
- Jean Tessier (1758-1840), 33, who eventually succeeded Nagot as superior in the U.S.;[5] and
- Michel Levadoux (1746-1815), 45, a more experienced Sulpician who had served at the Sulpician seminary in Limoges for seventeen years.

---

1 The exact date of Nagot's departure is a bit unclear, and some authors have chosen to say that he departed in the spring of 1791. The date chosen here is the date given by Nagot himself. See [Nagot?], "*Eglise Catholique du Maryland*," 132.

2 A brig is a two-masted, square-rigged sailing ship. A brig of 160 metric tons would have been rather small, with a deck about 70 ft. long and 20 ft. wide.

3 Chateaubriand, François-Auguste-René de, *Mémoires d'Outre-Tombe, Vol. I, in Ouevre Complète de Chateaubriand*, vol. XIII (Paris: Garnier Freres, 1904; reprinted, 1975) 310, n. 1, & 311, n. 1. (BnF)

4 Garnier served as superior general from 1826 to 1845.

5 Ruane, 32, wrote that Father Tessier was 43, but he was born in 1758. So he was 33.

Then, there were five seminarians, most with ties to Nagot: [6]

- Francis Tulloch (also spelled Tulloh and Tullow), 20, a former English soldier, reportedly converted by Nagot during his visit to England,[7] and a seminarian at Saint Sulpice whose confessor/director may have been Nagot.[8]
- John Floyd (d.1797), 26, another English seminarian, converted by John Thayer,[9] and recruited for the Sulpician Seminary in Paris by him and Nagot.[10]
- Pierre Joseph Perrineau (also spelled Périnault), 19, a seminarian from Montreal who was at the *Petit Séminaire*;
- John Edwards Caldwell (1769-1819), 22, an American who was probably converted by Edgeworth and who was probably also a new seminarian at Saint Sulpice in Paris;[11] and
- Jean-Édouard de Mondésir, 21, the French seminarian at the *Robertins* who was a penitent of Nagot, who had already been to Canada in 1790, and who gave us the memorable description of Nagot that will be cited below.[12]

---

6 For the ages of these seminarians, see Jean-Claude Berchet, *Chateaubriand* (Paris: Gallimard, 2012), 163-164.

7 Chateaubriand, *Mémoires d'Outre-Tombe*, 234. Chateaubriand got to know Tulloch well during the voyage, but it is not easy to imagine how Nagot was able to convert him during what is usually considered a brief visit to England in September 1790. Chateaubriand thought that Tulloch was easily influenced, but it may also be that he was ready for someone to give him a push. See also John Goldworth Alger, *Napoleon's British Visitors and Captives, 1801-1815* (New York: Pott, 1904), 70. However, Carroll believed that Tulloch was converted before his meeting with Nagot. See John Carroll, "Letter to Bishop Douglass, March 3, 1791" in *The Catholic Historical Review*, V (Apr. 1919-Jan. 1920), 396.

8 Ibid.

9 Campbell wrote that he was converted by Thayer. See Bernard U. Campbell, "Desultory Sketches of the Church in Maryland," *The Religious Cabinet*, I (Baltimore: John Murphy, 1842), 394. Diesbach wrote that Floyd was recruited in London by Nagot, presumably for the Sulpician seminary in Paris. See Ghislain de Diesbach, *Chateaubriand* (Paris: Perrin, 1998), 68

10 See http://catholicism.org/father-john-thayer.html (accessed 10/16/2015).

11 In Edgeworth, *Mémoires*, 36, there is reference to an American in the company of Lafayette who became a Catholic and entered the seminary as a result of his relationship with Edgeworth. In light of Carroll's letter of Oct. 12, 1791, we know that he was John Edwards [sic] Caldwell, the son of a American Presbyterian minister of Huguenot ancestry. In 1785, a few years after his parents' death, 14-year-old John Edwards was taken to France by the Marquis de Lafayette for his education. Caldwell was later converted in Paris (by Nagot?). See Hanley, I, 523. See also Kevin J. Hayes, *Jefferson in His Own Time: A Biographical Chronicle of His Life* (Iowa City: University of Iowa Press, 2012), 62.

12 Mondésir wrote his account at the request of Faillon in 1842. For excerpts from Mondésir's account, see Jean-Édouard de Mondésir, *Souvenirs d'Édouard de Mondésir* (Baltimore: Johns Hopkins, 1942). Some sections were translated and published as Jean de Mondésir, "Souveniers of Jean Edouard de Mondésir," in *The Voice of the Students and Alumni of St. Mary's Seminary* (Baltimore: St. Mary's Seminary, 1931), XI, No. 1 (Oct. 1931), 20-25; and XI, no. 2 (Nov., 1931), 23-24. The original manuscript is in the SAP in Materiaux, IV.

Finally, accompanying them was a priest-refugee of Nagot's vintage, Father Louis-César DeLavau (1741-1795), 50, who was a personal friend of Nagot and who was accompanied by his valet.[13] DeLavau had been a canon of the Basilica of Saint Martin of Tour and the treasurer of the chapter there, but in 1790 the Basilica had been nationalized and its canons had been dispersed.[14]

This date of departure is significant since it was at about the time of a major turning point in the French Revolution that led to the Terror. During the previous July, the revolutionary National Assembly, by this time augmented by some clergy and liberal nobles, had approved a controversial document called the Civil Constitution of the Clergy. It was aimed at reforming the Church in France in light of the ideals of the Revolution. It reduced the number of dioceses substantially and mandated salaries for the clergy.[15]

The belief that the French state had authority over important features of Church life had a very long history in France; it was an important part of what was eventually called Gallicanism.[16] In 1438 the basic principles of this approach were enshrined in The Pragmatic Sanction of Bourges, a document that was not acceptable to the Holy See mainly due to its conciliarist view of the Church. Nevertheless, this approach included practices that were common in Europe at the time. For example most bishops were elected by the canons of their cathedrals (often with political interference) and then the elections were confirmed by the pope.

In 1516 the ecclesiastical role of the French state was greatly enhanced when Pope Leo XII and King Francis I concluded the Concordat of Bologna. According to that agreement, which replaced the Pragmatic Sanction, the kings of France received the right to nominate 10 archbishops, 83 bishops and 127 abbots without the necessity of prior canonical elections. In return the king more clearly acknowledged the pope's authority, e.g., the need to obtain prior papal approval for the canonical installation of bishops.[17] In the following centuries, the crown became more and more involved in the administration of the Church, and important ecclesiastical offices were used as a rich resource for political patronage.

---

13 Mondésir, "Souveniers," 1st installment, 20. DeLavau (also De Lavau, or Delavau) was independently wealthy. He intended to pay for his own lodging in Baltimore. See Hanley, I, 516 and II, 41-42. See also. Herbermann, 19. The date of DeLavau's birth is from the *fichier généalogique* at the AMT.

14 The Basilica was used as a stable and a few years later it was demolished except for two 11th-century towers that still stand.

15 At Bishop Talleyrand's recommendation, the Assembly had already nationalized a large amount of ecclesiastical property and was auctioning it off as a way of reducing the huge national debt. This destroyed the benefice system, and so the Assembly had to find a way to compensate the clergy.

16 For more information on Gallicanism, see Kauffman, Ch. II.

17 At the time, this concession of power to the crown was very controversial in France because it violated older Gallican principles.

Another way that the crown was involved in Church administration was by use of "*la commende,*" another method of patronage. In medieval times, when an abbot or prior died, someone might be appointed *in commendam*, i.e., with income but without spiritual obligations, until a proper canonical election or appointment could be effected. However, in France during the *ancien régime*, commendatory appointments were usually permanent. Olier himself was the commendatory abbot of Pébrac and the commendatory prior of three priories. Talleyrand was made the commendatory abbot of a very rich monastery in Reims well before he was ordained a priest.

ABBEY OF PÉBRAC

There were many other ways that during the *ancien régime* the state intervened in ecclesiastical affairs. For example, the crown either closed non-viable monasteries or amalgamated them with viable ones. And the courts of law often adjudicated disputes over benefices and the feudal rights of the higher clergy. The courts were also instrumental in the suppression of the Jesuits in the 1760s.

So, from the perspective of its supporters, the Civil Constitution of the Clergy was not something completely novel – rather the new revolutionary government simply took on the traditional authority of the king.[18] When the

---

18 This was the position of the Oratorian Luc-François Lalande (1732-1805), a member of the National Assembly and later the constitutional bishop of Meurthe. By the publication of anonymous letters, Emery refuted his arguments in 1791. Emery contended that the realignment and suppression of dioceses by the Assembly was a usurpation of ecclesiastical authority. See Gosselin, II, 273ff.

Civil Constitution was presented to Louis XVI for his signature, he hesitated and sent it to Pope Pius VI for his approval. Yet, in December, 1790, and before the condemnation of the Civil Constitution was received from Rome, the leaders of the Revolution pressured the King into approving the administration of an oath to support the Civil Constitution. The government then mandated that every beneficed clergyman either take the oath or lose his office.

This oath caused most bishops and priests a crisis of conscience for two primary reasons. First, after the Assembly completely realigned the dioceses of France to coincide with departmental boundaries, the Civil Constitution, II.3, held that departmental administrative committees, which included elected lay officials, would appoint bishops and pastors. But, in some parts of France, these committees included Protestants and anticlerical agitators.[19] And, second, the Civil Constitution manifested a radical strain of Gallicanism in that it failed to acknowledge the authority of the Holy See. For example, II.17 did not require prior papal approval in order for there to be a valid canonical installation of a bishop by his metropolitan; and II.19 required only that the pope be notified of the selection of a bishop by the new bishop himself.[20] These provisions raised serious theological and pastoral concerns and violated a key requirement of the earlier settlement enshrined in the Concordat of Bologna.

As the oath began to be administered in January, 1791, Abbé Edgeworth described the situation to an Irish bishop who was a close friend:

> This morning was appointed for the taking of the oath in every parish church of Paris…At St. Sulpice the mob was outrageous. The curate…received 22 notes last night, by which he clearly saw there was a plan to get him murdered this morning, if he refused the oath…{H]is parishioners…saved his life from the villains who had been sent on purpose…Such is the position of this unfortunate town at the present moment.[21]

The oath led to a split of the clergy of France into those who took the oath (the jurors, or *prêtres insermentés*) and those who refused to take it (the non-jurors, or *prêtres assermentés*). Under the leadership of Emery, Nagot and all of the Sulpicians in France – one source says that there were 136 of them[22]– joined

---

19 Emery argued this point forcefully. See Méric, *Histoire*, 174-175, 177.
20 Gosselin, I, 242.
21 Woodgate, 37-38.
22 See Mathieu-Richard-Auguste Henrion, *Histoire des ordres religieux* (Brussels: La Société nationale pour la propagation des bon Livres, 1838), 291.

the latter category. [23] So in the January of 1791, Sulpician seminaries around France began to close.

Fortunately Nagot sailed to the U.S. in April, just before the pope's strong condemnation of the Civil Constitution was finally made public. Had Nagot waited only a few months, he would have become a target of those who were coming to see the non-jurors, or recusants, as counter-revolutionaries. [24] In June, while Nagot was still sailing on the North Atlantic, the King and Queen (along with Madame Élisabeth) tried unsuccessfully to flee from France. They were apprehended at Varennes and returned to Paris under armed escort. The revolutionary government confined them to the Tuileries Palace and put even more pressure on non-jurors to swear to uphold the Civil Constitution of the Clergy.

THE FLIGHT OF THE ROYAL FAMILY TO VARENNES (BNF)

---

23 Pasquier recently described the French Sulpicians as moderate Gallicans who were "tightly integrated into ecclesiastical hierarchy and authority." He says that they brought this perspective to the U.S. and so were not inclined to "a 'republican' form of Catholicism." Michael Pasquier, *Fathers on the Frontier: French Missionaries and the Roman Catholic Priesthood in the United States, 1789-1870* (New York: Oxford, 2010), 30-31. Pasquier does not mention Father Olier's great respect for the See of Peter that is still part of the Sulpician tradition. This tradition must have contributed to the Sulpicians' stance against the Oath. The kind of moderate Gallicanism espoused by the Sulpicians is explained in some detail by Kauffman, Ch. II.

24 Recall that this was the reason for Currateau's death. For more information on this change of attitude, see Tackett, 547-551.

In September of 1791, Edgeworth described the deteriorating situation in another letter:

> Our house [i.e., the Missions Étrangères de Paris on the rue du Bac] subsists still, but in a few days perhaps it will share the fate of all other religious establishments and fall to the ground. The plan of the committee has lately been published. St. Sulpice, St. Lazare, St. Nicholas, Missions Étrangères, etc., etc., to say all in a word, every ecclesiastical corporation in France is to be suppressed according to this plan, and reduced to the same footings with the regular ones [i.e., the religious congregations], which, as you know, were suppressed a year ago.[25]

PORT OF ST. MALO c. 1770 (BnF)

A few months later, DuBourg was forced to flee from Issy, and the Blessed Sulpician martyrs were put to death in Paris. If Nagot had still been in Paris at that time, his non-juring status and royalist connections would probably have led to his death. As it was, Mondésir wrote that Nagot and his traveling companions were arrested at the port of St. Malo before they could sail, but fortunately they were released through the merciful intervention of an unnamed juring priest who was serving on the local revolutionary committee.[26]

---

25 Woodgate, 59-60. Most religious communities had been disbanded except for those involved in what was considered socially useful activity, e.g., teaching and nursing. The government saw no social value in allowing contemplative and monastic communities to continue, and besides, the government needed their assets.

26 Mondésir, "Souveniers," 1st installment, 21.

We have some interesting information about Father Nagot during his three-month voyage to the New World. A good part of it comes from writings of two of his fellow voyagers. The first of these was the author François-Auguste-René, vicomte de Chateaubriand (1768-1848),[27] who was also distancing himself from the Revolution.[28] The second source was Mondésir who was eventually ordained in the United States.[29]

THE YOUNG CHATEAUBRIAND

Chateaubriand's account includes his initial positive impression of Father Nagot: "a talented man."[30] Chateaubriand recounted that later in the voyage Nagot was weakened so much by seasickness during the crossing that he had to be carried ashore when the *Saint-Pierre* stopped briefly at the French island of Saint Pierre off the south coast of Newfoundland.[31] Chateaubriand also thought that Nagot had some reservations about his skeptical state of mind because Nagot kept a close eye on Chateaubriand's developing friendship with the new convert Tulloch. This seems to have irritated Chateaubriand.[32]

Mondésir's account tells us more about Nagot during the voyage. When he was able, he led his companions in their daily prayers and devotions. They travelled during the Lenten and Easter seasons. At one point he allowed Chateaubriand, who was not particularly devout by his own admission, to read to the group. However, afterwards Nagot criticized Chateaubriand's performance, saying, "[A]n ascetical book should not be declaimed in a tone which befitted a

27 Chateaubriand was about the same age as the seminarians traveling with Nagot.

28 "*Je fis marché avec un capitaine nommé Dujardin. Il devait transporter à Baltimore l'abbé Nagot, supérieur du séminaire de Saint-Sulpice, et plusieurs séminaristes, sous la conduite de leur chef.*" Chateaubriand, *Mémoires*, 310.

29 His recollections were written in 1842 at the request of Sulpician historian Father Michel Faillon, a biographer of Father Emery.

30 "*J'avais pour compagnons de voyage des jeunes séminaristes de Saint-Sulpice, que leur supérieur, homme de mérite, conduisait à Baltimore.*" See François René de Chateaubriand, "*Voyage en Amérique*" in *Oeuvres Complètes de M. le Vicomte de Chateaubriand*, XI (Paris: Pourrat Frères, 1834), 6.

31 Chateaubriand, *Mémoires*, 342.

32 "*Il [Chateaubriand] a raconté dans une note de l'Essai sur les révolutions, chapitre LIV, comment il avait essayé d'entraîner le jeune converti et de l'arracher à la domination de M. Nagot.*" See Mondésir, *Souvenir*, 19, n. 2.

tragedy."[33] Needless to say, Chateaubriand did not read again. At another time, Nagot allowed him to make some personal remarks at Stations of the Cross, but Mondésir implied that Nagot regretted it afterwards.

Mondésir also gives us the following colorful image of Nagot's state of health. Nagot was "like a carp out of water: silent and almost dead, he spent almost every day lying on his bunk."[34] On a more upbeat note, Mondésir described a sermon that Nagot gave in a church on the island of Saint Pierre:

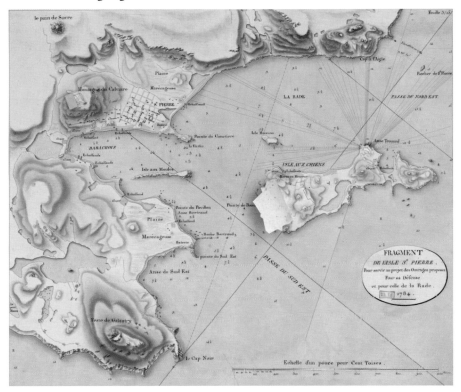

THE HARBOR AND TOWN OF THE ISLAND OF SAINT-PIERRE C. 1784 (BNF)

> Father Nagot had much soul, enthusiasm and exaltation. He announced that we were going to convert America; and there is no doubt that he ardently desired to do so....[A]t the Grand Séminare....I often heard that Father Emery sought to calm him, his directeur du [sic], who had the fire of a young man.[35]

33 Mondésir, "Souveniers," 1st installment, 21. The French original was, "*M. Nagot lui fit observer un jour qu'un livre ascétique ne se déclamait pas sur le ton de la tragédie.*" See Mondésir, *Souvenirs*, 20.

34 "*M. Nagot...presque toujours gisait sur son grabat, comme une carpe hors de l'eau, sans parole et presque sans vie.* See Mondésir, *Souvenirs*, 31.

35 Ibid, 22. See Ch. VI, n. 5, above. Nagot is also given this abbreviated title in a note written by Father Courtade. See "*Note de M. Courtade,* in *Matériaux* , IV, 903.

In this context, it is appropriate to note that Mondésir recalled some sage advice that John Carroll gave to Nagot later on: "If one was to succeed in breaking for Americans the bread of life, one must make the dough with one bushel of zeal for nine bushels of prudence."[36]

In another context, Mondésir said that he was reciting the breviary with Nagot and tried to pronounce his Latin with an English accent. "It was as though I had given a blow to the holy old man; he returned it *motu primo* with a good knock, 'Away with young Anglomania!'"[37] Then Mondésir added, "Fr. Nagot seldom put aside his serious and reserved manner; as soon as he perceived that he did not have it, he quickly came back to it." For this reason Mondésir confessed that he was more comfortable with Garnier who was less intense and more outgoing.

In addition to these reports from Chateaubriand and Mondésir, we have a letter from Nagot himself, probably written to Emery, that was published in a French periodical early in 1792, just as the French Revolution was turning violently anticlerical.[38] Most of what he wrote was merely an objective description of the voyage itself. However, in a few places, he gives us a glimpse of his leadership of the group of emigrés. During the voyage, for example, he saw that there was a steady regimen of prayer, some of it sung and some of it Marian. Four times a day, there were prayer services, with hymns. Vespers was celebrated in common, and Mass was celebrated on Sundays and other days of obligation.

Nagot noted that three of his fellow priests, DeLavau, Levadoux, and Garnier enjoyed good health and were able to lead the Holy Week observances. This comment indirectly confirms Chateaubriand's and Mondésir's observation that Nagot himself suffered greatly from seasickness. Nagot also wrote that it was very cold as they approached the Grand Banks and that the passengers were very eager ("*plus volontier*") to stop at the Island of Saint Pierre in order to get some clean drinking water. He added demurely, "I had a great need to breathe terrestrial air."[39] While there, he and his companions assisted at the local parish.

---

36 "*Monseigneur…hâta de dire à Mr. Nagot, que pour rompre aux Américains le pain de la parole de Dieu, il fallait faire de la <u>mouture</u> avec un boisseau de zèle, sur neuf boisseaux de prudence.*" Mondésir, *Souvenirs*, 27.

37 Mondésir, "Souveniers," 1st installment, 23.

38 Anonymous, "*Eglise Catholique du Maryland*," 129-147. This journal reviewed important developments in the Church in France and in the foreign missions. It seems reasonable to think that Father Emery or one of his close associates composed and submitted this article. If so, a passage on page 129 might explain the Society's priorities with respect to conversion in the United States, a topic that, according to Mondésir, was the subject of Nagot's impassioned sermon on the island of Saint Pierre. Not only was the effort aimed at the conversion of Protestants, but part of it was the reconversion of Catholics living in remote areas who were not practicing their faith because of the lack of priests to serve them. (Today we would call this new evangelization.) This article seemed to be a subtle invitation to French priests to come to the U.S. This letter was later republished in Gaspard-André-Joseph Jauffret, *Mémoires pour servir* à *l'histoire de la religion* à *la fin du XVIIIe siècle* (Paris: Le Clère, 1803), 407-408. See also Emery, "Counsels and Rules," para. 1.

39 "*J'avais un grand besoin de respirer l'air de terre.*" Anonymous, "*Eglise Catholique du Maryland*," 135.

He wrote that it was a great consolation for his party to attend Eucharistic devotion on the island after so many days at sea, and he confirmed that he preached at the local parish on Ascension Thursday.

Finally, Nagot wrote that while on the island of Saint Pierre he tried to convert some English Protestants who were forced to land there due to an accident at sea. He wrote that all in his party were quite optimistic about the outcome of this effort.[40]

---

40 "*Nous avons dans le moment le plus grande espérance du succès.*" Anonymous, "*Eglise Catholique du Maryland,*" 136. We do not know the outcome.

Part Two
THE UNITED STATES

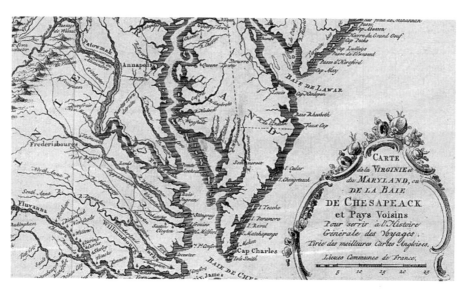

FRENCH MAP OF THE CHESAPEAKE BAY, 1780

THE NEW WORLD

In July 1791 the *Saint-Pierre* rounded Cape Charles and entered the Chesapeake Bay. It is interesting that the first two incidents in the U.S. that Nagot described had to do with religion. He began by noting that, when a Bay pilot came aboard to take over control of the ship, it prompted him to say to himself, "What a shame that these people are not Catholic."[1] But Nagot added that he was comforted shortly afterwards when he learned that the pilot was indeed a member of the Church. Then, Nagot reported that, after sailing part way up the Bay, unfavorable winds and the need for provisions forced the ship to lie at anchor on the shore of Maryland for three days. During that time, some passengers went ashore, including Chateaubriand and DeLavau. With the assistance of a translator, DeLavau had a conversation with a 64-year-old American merchant-farmer. Nagot reported that what was most surprising about this conversation was both the man's positive attitude toward Catholicism, even though he was not Catholic, and his lack of interest in the Protestantism of most of his neighbors.[2]

These two incidents show that Nagot and his companions were aware that they had entered a world with a very different culture and history from the world they had left behind. For example, Chateaubriand recalled later that, on going ashore, he was in "a republic of a kind unknown then, announcing a change in the human mind and the political order."[3] And Mondésir, who may also have gone ashore, wrote that arrival in the U.S. entailed "the surprise and the shock of another civilization" (*"la surprise et le choc d'une autre civilization"*).[4]

Nagot's narrative prompts three reflections on the country he was entering. First, the religious landscape was very different: the United States was one of the most religiously diverse countries in the western world. Catholics were a tiny minority (only about 30,000 out of about 4,000,000), and most of them lived in the mid-Atlantic region, once called the middle colonies. These colonies had been especially tolerant and were inhabited mainly by Anglicans, Presbyterians (some of them from Scotland and France), Methodists, Quakers, Lutherans (mostly from Germany), and successors of the Left Wing of the Reformation (also from Germany). Catholics (mostly English, but with some Irish and Germans) were found mainly in the rural areas of Maryland and Pennsylvania. Prior to the American Revolution, New England had been dominated by English Congregationalists and other dissenters (from the Church of England), and

---

1 Anonymous, *"Eglise Catholique du Maryland,"* 136.

2 Ibid., 137-138.

3 François-René de Chateaubriand, *Chateaubriand's Travels in America,* trans. R. Switzer (Lexington, KY: University of Kentucky Press, 1969), 12.

4 Mondésir, *Souvenirs,* 2.

Catholics were not welcome.[5] In the south, the Church of England dominated religious life. Slaves, though numerous, had little influence at the time.

Even in Maryland, which had been established by the Irish-English Catholic George Calvert, the First Lord Baltimore, as a place of refuge for Catholics, the majority of citizens were never Catholic. Thus, after the founding of the colony, Cecil Calvert, the Second Lord Baltimore, decreed religious toleration.[6] Calvert's attitude has been described as follows:

> Elizabeth I justified her persecution of Catholics on the grounds that a nation state could not endure the strain of two religions within its borders. A generation later, Calvert had come to believe that the forcing of a conscience could be even more destructive of the common weal.[7]

LORD BALTIMORE ISSUES THE EDICT OF TOLERATION

---

5 At the time of Nagot's arrival, there were only about 100 Catholics in Boston.

6 For more on the early history of Maryland, see Robert J. Brugger, *Maryland: A Middle Temperament: 1634-1980* (Baltimore: Johns Hopkins, 1988).

7 Thomas W. Spalding, *The Premier See: A History of the Archdiocese of Baltimore, 1789-1994* (Baltimore: Johns Hopkins, 1989), 1. In this sense, Elizabeth I was similar to Louis XIV who revoked the Edict of Nantes in France.

Maryland's colonial regime of toleration was permanently ended in 1689, at the time of England's Glorious Revolution, and the Church of England became the established Church in the colony. So, prior to the American Revolution, the religious situation for Catholics in the Maryland was similar to their situation in England, and educated Catholics of Maryland were drawn to the writings of contemporary Catholic missionaries in England like Bishop Richard Challoner (1691-1781).[8] At the same time, the penal laws were not as rigorously enforced in Maryland, a place founded by Catholics. So the situation in colonial Maryland was almost the reverse of that in France after the revocation of the Edict of Nantes. Here a Protestant majority set limits on the rights of a Catholic minority.[9]

BISHOP CHALLONER

Nevertheless, being a small minority turned out to have its advantages. The Church was not entangled with the colonial regime in the way that the Church in France was entangled with the French monarchy. By way of contrast, American members of the Church of England faced a crisis during the American Revolution caused by the disestablishment of their denomination. Many Anglican clergy and other Anglicans left the country. Those who remained had to declare independence from the motherland, to change the name of their denomination, and, after the war, to establish their own hierarchy without help from the Anglican Church in England.[10]

Moreover, the Founding Fathers of the U.S., though "enlightened," had no animus toward organized religion[11] and accepted the deep religiosity of many of their fellow citizens. So the American Revolution did not have the destructive impact on Catholicism that the French Revolution had in France, and by and large American Catholics followed in the footsteps of the wealthy Charles Carroll of Carrollton (1737-1832) and welcomed the American Revolution and the religious toleration that it brought. "There were virtually no Catholic loyalists in Maryland."[12]

---

8 See, for example, Margaret M. Reher, *Catholic Intellectual Life in America* (New York: Macmillan, 1989), 10.

9 The status of Catholics in colonial America has recently been treated extensively in Robert Emmett Curran's *Papist Devils: Catholics in British America, 1574-1783* (Washington, DC: Catholic Univerity of America, 2014).

10 They eventually got a bishop of the Church of Scotland to ordain a bishop for them.

11 For more background, see Martin E. Marty, "The American Revolution and Religion, 1765-1815," in *The Cambridge History of Christianity*, VII, eds. S. Brown and T. Tackett. (Cambridge, UK: Cambridge Univerity Press, 2006). However, not all of the founding fathers were unprejudiced about Catholicism.

12 Curran, *Papist Devils*, 257.

CHARLES CARROLL OF CARROLLTON

The result was an unusually tolerant society for the time. In his recollections, Mondésir expressed amazement at this.[13] He wrote that there was less conflict between Catholics and Protestants in the U.S. than between Jansenists and Molinists in France.[14] He also noted that Bishop Carroll had good relations with the local Episcopal bishop and that they dined together. This environment must have seemed quite strange at first to Nagot and his French companions.[15]

---

13 Mondésir, *Souvenirs*, 48.

14 Molinism was the name of a theological school named after the 16th-century Spanish Jesuit Luis de Molina (1535-1600). The Jansenist movement considered Molinism to be a new form of Pelagianism, the heresy fought by St. Augustine more than a thousand years earlier.

15 An unnamed voyager with Nagot wrote that they found themselves among so many sects with churches ("*des temples*") more impressive than the little Catholic church ("*l'église*") in Baltimore. See Anonymous, "*Eglise Catholique du Maryland*," 140. The modest Catholic church would have been St. Peter's, the pro-cathedral. The distinction between Catholic "churches" and Protestant "temples" was characteristically French.

For instance, Nagot thought it was worth noting that, shortly after his arrival in Baltimore, he and his companions were on their way to vespers at Baltimore's only Catholic church when they were approached by a vested Episcopal minister for a conversation. [16]

Nevertheless, in 1791 and in the decades that followed, there was still suspicion about Catholics in many parts of the nation, especially in New England. As one historian has put it, "In a world flooded by bigotry, in which Rome was perceived as Babylon and where *Foxe's Book of Martyrs* remained a favorite text, the small band of American Catholics was not inclined to declare its official existence, especially its Roman ties."[17] And it was one of Carroll's priorities to present the Church as consistently respectable and fully American. That is one reason why he fought against ethnic division inside the Catholic community: it would draw attention to the increasingly foreign-born membership of the Church and perhaps raise questions about the patriotism of Catholics. Interestingly, as we shall see, Nagot soon adapted to the approach advocated by Carroll, including his tolerant attitude toward Protestants.[18]

Second, not only did DeLavau's friendly encounter with the American merchant-farmer underline the religious differences between the U.S. and the *ancien régime* but it also showed that the politics here were very different. Prior to the American Revolution, Frenchmen like Nagot and DeLavau would not have been welcome in Maryland. During the French and Indian War that led to dire consequences for the French monarchy, anti-Catholicism reached a peak in the thirteen colonies.[19] France was seen as synonymous with two evils that were alien to British colonial values: absolutism and popery.[20] As early as 1744 in Maryland, Catholics were dismissed from the militia and disarmed,[21] and during the war, in some of the colonies, extra taxes were levied on Catholics.[22] They were seen as a kind of fifth column. This paranoia only began to decline after the fall of Quebec to the British in 1759.

One French priest who served as a chaplain during the American Revolution described a typical American stereotype of the French as follows: the French

---

16 Ibid., 142.

17 Dolores Liptak, *Immigrants and Their Church* (New York: Macmillan, 1989), 4.

18 In the second chapter of his work, Kauffman explained how the Sulpicians and Carroll had similar views of the Church, but the kind of religious toleration practiced in this country must have been a stretch for Nagot, at least at first.

19 Curran, *Papist Devils*. Ch. 9.

20 In fact, later on the Founding Fathers were inspired by the writings of Radical Whigs who saw too many vestiges of absolutism in the British system of government, and the American Revolution was motivated partly by charges of absolutism, i.e., overriding of the traditional rights of English citizens, in the British colonial system.

21 Ibid., 204.

22 See, for example, ibid., 221-222.

"live under the yoke of despotism, indulged in prejudices and superstition, almost pagan in their religion; like deformed frivolous machines, unreliable and inconsistent, occupied only with the care of curling their hair and making up their faces; without delicacy, without faith, and disrespectful of the most sacred duties."[23]

By 1791, however, Nagot and his companions were more than welcome in the United States, and especially in Maryland. Not only had American Catholics proved patriotic during the Revolution but the old enemy France had come to the aid of the colonials. Liberal French aristocrats like Rochambeau and Lafayette were heroes in the eyes of most Americans. So, though relations between the U.S. and France would sour again later, as we shall see, 1791 was a particularly favorable time for the French Sulpicians to begin their new mission in the U.S.[24]

THE MARQUIS DE LAYAFETTE

23 Gregory A. Wood, *The French Presence in Maryland: 1524-1800* (Baltimore: Gateway Press, 1978), 93.

24 Curran points out that just as France had been a place of refuge for British Catholics during the English Reformation, now a small former British colony, Maryland, was a place of refuge for French Catholics during the French Revolution. See ibid., 281.

Thirdly and finally, Nagot's account of DeLavau's encounter reminds us of another difference, the difference of language between France and the U.S. Nagot wrote that DeLavau knew only a few words of English.[25] He would never be happy in the U.S. mainly because he, in his 50s, found it very difficult to master the language.

We have already seen that Nagot himself did know some English, at least enough to translate Thayer's account of his conversion and to communicate with some native English speakers.[26] But even in Nagot's case – and here age was also a factor – his imperfect command of spoken English proved to be something of a hindrance to his ministry in the U.S.[27]

In any case, Nagot and most of his companions sensed that they had entered a world that had a different religious history, a different political experience, and a different language from their homeland.

On Sunday, July 10, as the travelers arrived in Baltimore, more specifically in the section of Baltimore called Fells Point, they must have also immediately sensed that they had come into a society that was also starkly different in terms of physical and economic development. During the 18th century the area around Baltimore harbor had become known for shipping and the milling of grain. Gradually three small communities (Baltimore Town, Jones Town and Fells Point) merged to form greater Baltimore Town. In 1791 it was already the fastest growing community in the U.S. and one of the largest.[28] Nevertheless, it had only about 15,000 inhabitants and no significant architecture.[29] So arriving there would have been a great comedown from Paris that, in 1791, had more than half a million inhabitants and boasted some of the most impressive monumental buildings in the world like the Louvre, Notre-Dame Cathedral, and Les Invalides.

Nevertheless, Chateaubriand recalled much later that, upon reaching their destination, they were encouraged by what they saw:

---

25 *"[C]elui-ci ne sachant encore que quelques mots Anglois."* See Anonymous, *"Eglise Catholique du Maryland,"* 137.

26 Herbermann thought that Nagot had to "acquire a new language" at the age of 60. See Herbermann, 56.

27 See [Garnier?], *L'ami de la Religion*, 287. The same was not true in the case of Garnier because he was young and very talented in languages.

28 Robert E. Curran, *The Bicentennial History of Georgetown University*, I (Washington, DC: Georgetown, 1993), 22.

29 In 1790 Maryland had only about 120,000 inhabitants. About 33% of these were slaves living mostly in southern Maryland and on the eastern shore. See Brugger, 781. Baltimore continued to grow rapidly, and by 1808, the population would be about 40,000. At that point, Baltimore was a more important port than Boston. See Annabelle M. Melville, *Elizabeth Ann Seton: 1774-1821*, ed. Betty Ann McNeil (Hanover, PA: Sheridan Press, 2009), 178.

Baltimore offered herself to us as on the edge of a lake. Opposite the city rose a hill shaded with trees, at the foot of which they were beginning to build a few homes....Baltimore did not have then the extent that it has today [i.e., 1827] It was a very pretty, clean, and animated city.[30]

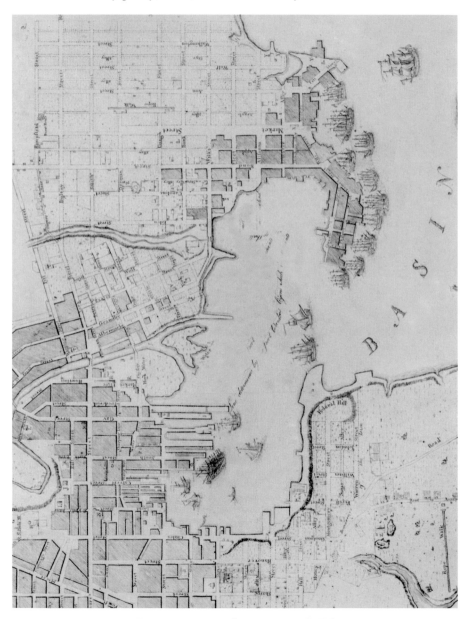

BALTIMORE IN 1792 (COURTESY OF MDHS)

30 Chateaubriand, *Travels*, 13-14.

X
A Promising Start

After disembarking, Nagot and his companions were warmly greeted by the rector of Saint Peter's, the modest pro-cathedral and Baltimore's only parish, and by representatives of the local Catholic community – Carroll was out of town.[1] The voyagers stayed in temporary quarters for several days while Nagot located a suitable permanent dwelling for them.[2] This building, a two and a half story inn called The One Mile Tavern, was located in an undeveloped area, a good distance from the hustle and bustle of the harbor. This inn became what was later called St. Mary's Seminary.[3]

SAINT PETER'S PRO-CATHEDRAL

At first, the One Mile Tavern was rented, but soon Nagot, with assistance from Carroll, was able to purchase the Tavern along with four acres. This purchase consumed over a third of the funds that were left over after all of the expenses of the voyage were paid off.

---

1 St. Peter's Churc, which resembled a house, was built in 1770 and served mostly a small community of Acadian Catholics who had been expelled from Nova Scotia during the French and Indian War. Starting in 1789 it served as the pro-cathedral until the Cathedral of the Assumption of the Blessed Virgin Mary was completed in 1821.

2 Faillon wrote that Nagot thought that the first location was too close to the "*le tumult*" of the city and so he looked for a place that was more remote ("*plus solitaire*"). See Faillon, *Histoire*, I, 37.

3 It was first called "The Seminary of Saint Sulpice," like its mother seminary in Paris. In the 184, it began to use "St. Mary's" in the title. Apparently this name was adopted from the College and the Chapel. This study will use "St. Mary's Seminary" throughout.

THE ONE MILE TAVERN

On July 18, 1791, Nagot moved everyone into the inn and then directed their attention to the conversion of a room into a chapel that he blessed and dedicated to the Blessed Virgin Mary. There the first celebration of Mass took place on July 20, probably led by Nagot.[4] The next day, Carroll returned to Baltimore and received the group with great joy and warmth. They then began to prepare the facility for the opening of school on the 3ʳᵈ of October.[5] On July 26, Nagot wrote to Emery that they were focusing their energy entirely on building a spiritual edifice:[6] he intended to recreate the environment of Paris' Seminary of Saint Sulpice on this side of the Atlantic. [7]

In this context, it is revealing to note that, among Nagot's personal effects, are three bound, undated books in French that were written in his own hand. They have the following long title: "The Spirit and Maxims of M. Olier on Seminaries, on Those Who Are Being Prepared There for Priesthood, or Those Who Have Already Attained It, on the Directors Who Govern, and on the Bishops Who

4 Ruane, 35.

5 Herbermann, 23. After one more year they adopted a more American academic calendar and opened in early September.

6 Ibid., 140.

7 Nagot wrote to Emery on August 28 that the various furnishings were so expensive that he only purchased what was strictly necessary. See Anonymous, *"Eglise Catholique du Maryland,"* 141.

Are Its First Superiors."[8] These books contain selections from the writings of Olier that Nagot had included as a kind of appendix to his not-yet-published *Life of Mr. Olier, Pastor of Saint Sulpice.*[9] He probably wrote these short books not long after he arrived in the U.S. to inspire his confreres and explain to other interested parties the Sulpician approach to priestly formation.[10]

In this context, it is also interesting to note that, not long after arriving in Baltimore, Nagot learned from Carroll that there was a new French Carmelite monastery in Port Tobacco, Maryland. So, imitating Olier's request to the canons at the Basilica of Tours, Nagot wrote to the Carmelites, proposing a union of prayer and good works between them and the new Seminary in Baltimore.[11] After the agreement was signed, seminarians sometimes visited the sisters to ask for prayers.

So Nagot's beginning in the U.S. held great promise despite the newness of the environment and the constraints imposed by somewhat limited financial resources.[12] Nagot was energized by the task at hand. In his August 28, 1791, letter to Emery, he wrote, despite everything, "We are too happy here."[13] Carroll also was delighted with the presence and conduct of the Sulpicians and so informed the Holy See a few months later: "The remarkable piety of these priests is admirable, and their example is a stimulant and spur to all who feel themselves called to work in the vineyard of the Lord."[14]

---

8 *"Esprit et maximes de M. Olier sur les Séminaires, sur eux qui s'y Préparent au Sacerdoce, ou qui y sont déjà parvenus, sur les Directeurs qui les gouvernent, et les Évêques qui en sont les premiers Supérieurs."*

9 In Nagot's day, handwritten copies were a common way of reproducing written materials that were not available.

10 One copy is inscribed, "Found in a Boston store by Rev. Francis Havey." Havey was a Sulpician who served at St. John's Seminary in Boston in the late 19th century. So this copy may have found its way to Boston to serve as a resource for the Sulpicians who were the first faculty of St. John's Seminary, but then it was sold after the Sulpicians left St. John's.

11 See C. W. Currier, *Carmel in America 1790-1890* (Darien, IL: Carmelite Press, 1989), 77 and 82.

12 Nagot also initiated the process to become a naturalized citizen in 1791. In 1792 pro-French Maryland made naturalization of French citizens easier. See Gordon Wood, *The French Presence,* 143 and 144. Nagot's certificate of naturalization was granted in 1794. See Naturalization Certificate for F. C. Nagot, Nov. 17, 1794 (Baltimore, handwritten court document in Father Nagot's personal papers in the collection of the Associated Sulpicians of the U.S. at the AA, 1794).

13 Ibid., 141.

14 Ibid., 36.

Early on, Nagot was also encouraged by the support given by Emery. In the spring and summer of 1792, he sent Nagot six more Sulpicians, mostly young, (Fathers Jean-Baptiste Chicoisneau, Jean-Baptiste David, Benoît-Joseph Flaget, Ambrose Maréchal, Gabriel Richard, and François Ciquard) and two more seminarians, including Stephen Badin, the first alumnus of St. Mary's Seminary to be ordained. To implement the original plan of 1790, Carroll and Nagot then sent Levadoux and three of the newcomers (Ciquard, Flaget, and Richard) to minister to Catholics where once French Canadian priests had served as missionaries. Emery considered this to be in the spirit of Father Olier and Father Bretonvilliers who had such concern for evangelization in New France. Emery also hoped that a college or academy could be opened in Illinois or elsewhere on the frontier that might prepare some students to enter the seminary in Baltimore.[15]

---

15 Faillon, *Histoire*, I, 49. Richard, for example, took on this task when he got to Detroit.

XI
YEARS OF DISAPPOINTMENT AND CONFLICT
1792-1801

It would be beyond the scope of this study to discuss the full range of early Sulpician ministries in the United States. Historian have already done that. Rather the primary focus here will be on Nagot's experiences and perspectives during this period insofar as we know them.

What is important to keep in mind is that there was a kind of division of labor among the early Sulpicians. Most of Nagot's younger Sulpician companions came and went from the Seminary and most of them served, at least for a time, as missionaries in various parts of the U.S. Moreover, two (Flaget and DuBourg) were named bishops during Nagot's lifetime. Nagot himself, however, remained at the Seminary until 1806 and he devoted all of his energy to ensuring its future. The only other Sulpician who remained at the Seminary during Nagot's entire tenure as superior was Tessier, his confidant and right-hand man.[1] Consequently, it was Nagot who was primarily responsible for the survival and growth of St. Mary's Seminary.

FATHER TESSIER

As the title of this section implies, the first ten years would be very hard years for Nagot. After almost a quarter century of acknowledged success at the Seminary of Saint Sulpice in Paris, he would undergo what was probably the most difficult period of his life. The main source of difficulty would be lack of resources, both people and funding. As often happens, inadequate resources create competition, conflict, and setbacks, and these, in turn, place a special burden on the one with the most responsibility for the success of the mission.

---

1 Mondésir wrote that Tessier was Nagot's "faithful Achates." Achates was the loyal companion of Aeneas in Virgil's *Aeneid*, and Mondésir believed that Tessier was the only one with whom Nagot shared his personal disappointments. See Mondésir, "Souveniers," 2nd Installment, 23.

Low Enrollment

For the first ten years, the root problem was lack of people, more specifically, poor seminary enrollment, mainly due to the lack of native vocations. As was already noted, this was anticipated to some extent, and so Nagot brought five seminarians with him, three of whom were native English-speakers. However, including these five, a total of only eighteen seminarians would be enrolled at St. Mary's during this ten-year period. Of these, only seven would be ordained priests, and most of these were not native-born Americans.

Moreover, most of the first five original seminarians, in whom Nagot had invested much hope, did not become priests. And those who were ordained, did not serve as priests in the U.S. for long. Tulloch, Nagot's protégé, left the seminary after only one year,[2] returned to England and eventually married.[3] Caldwell, under the influence of his family, left the seminary after only a short time and returned to Calvinism.[4] He would eventually became the first general

agent of the American Bible Society and publisher of *The Christian Herald*.[5] Perrineau, who would soon learn English well, was attached to his family and went back to Canada after only two years in Baltimore. He was then ordained for the Diocese of Quebec.[6] In addition, Floyd, who was ordained a priest in 1795 and who did very well at the beginning of his ministry, died of disease two years later. And Mondésir, finally ordained

JOHN EDWARDS CALDWELL   a priest in 1798, returned to France in 1801.

The early losses of Tulloch and Caldwell must have been particularly discouraging for Nagot who, as we have already seen, had a special affinity for converts because he shared their fervor. Already in the fall of 1791, Carroll wrote to his friend Plowden that Nagot "placed the utmost dependence" on Caldwell but that he, Carroll, thought that Caldwell might not return to the seminary after he renewed contact with his family.[7]

Nagot, of course, felt the loss of other seminarians as well. As Carroll wrote to Emery in August 1800:

---

2 Hanley, II, 40.

3 See Victor Girard, "*Chateaubriand à vingt-deux ans: d'après des documents iné*dits" in *Le Correspondent*, CCXX (1905), 587. [583-594]

4 Anonymous, "John Edwards Caldwell: First Agent General of the American Bible Society," in *Bible Society Record*, 51 (February 1906), 28.

5 Ibid. In 1794 Caldwell reimbursed the Sulpicians for the cost of his voyage from Paris to Baltimore. See Ruane, 68.

6 Hanley, II, 42, 89, and 109.

7 Hanley, I, 523.

The news that Father Nagot gives me of the house has truly saddened me. He tells me that there is not a single subject for the diocese at the seminary, and that there is little hope of having a greater number in the future: in fine, that subjects that seemed to show dispositions for the clerical state and on whom we believed we could count, were turned aside at a moment when it was least expected.[8]

Why, in addition to the fact that the Catholic population was small, did Nagot face such a shortage of seminarians at this time? After all, 36 sons of Catholic families had joined the Jesuits during the half century preceding the American Revolution.[9] So why were there so few native vocations in the 1790s? Not all of the reasons for this are known, but two things are clear. First, most of those who had joined the Jesuits during the generation prior to the American Revolution were alumni of Jesuit-run colleges in northern France and in the Low Countries, Saint Omer's College being the most prominent. Both Leonard Neale (1746-1817) and Carroll were alumni of that institution. However, the Jesuits lost those colleges at the time of their suppression in France, and in the 1790s the revolutionary situation in Europe discouraged well-to-do Catholic families from sending their sons there for studies.

SAINT OMER'S COLLEGE
(ARCHIVES OF PAS-DE-CALAIS)

Second, as Carroll had pointed out to Emery and Nagot back in 1790, there was, as of yet, no Catholic academy or college in the U.S. that could substitute for the Jesuit colleges in Europe and that could prepare men to enter a major seminary. To put it another way, there was no institution in the U.S. like the College of Tours that Nagot himself had attended. So for him the primary objective during his years as superior in the U.S. was to find or create a school that would become a productive feeder for the seminary. This task, along with the need to find financial support, absorbed most of Nagot's energy during his first ten years here. By 1800, Nagot was so frustrated at the Seminary's lack of

8 Hanley, II, 313.
9 Curran, *The Bicentennial History*, I, 7.

enrollment, that he wrote to Emery that there was no hope for its future.[10]

Conflict with Former Jesuits

In order to develop a viable feeder institution, Nagot, following Carroll, first placed his hope in Georgetown, which opened in November 1791, just one month after St. Mary's. But Georgetown itself struggled to survive in its early years, and only one graduate of that institution entered the Seminary during its first decade of St. Mary's operation.[11] Moreover, Nagot's efforts to support Georgetown met distrust and sometimes led to conflict with the former Jesuits who were its trustees. This weighed on Nagot as the leader of the Sulpicians and a grateful Jesuit alumnus.

FATHER WHITE BAPTIZES A
NATIVE AMERICAN CHIEF

To appreciate what happened, it is necessary to know a bit about the history of the Jesuits in Maryland.[12] The first three Jesuits, led by Father Andrew White, came from England to shores of the Chesapeake Bay as missionaries on March 25, 1634, along with the first colonists sent by Lord Baltimore, the Lord Proprietor of Maryland. So the Jesuits had been in Maryland for more than a century and a half when the Sulpicians arrived.[13]

The Lord Proprietor saw Maryland as a colonial version of rural northern England where a relatively small number of Catholics lived in relative peace with many Protestant landholders and farm laborers. So he offered land grants to many of the colonists in return for a promise of annual payments. Some of the more prominent Catholic settlers received very generous grants.

---

10 Thomas W. Spalding, *John Carroll Recovered* (Baltimore: Cathedral Foundation, 2000), 45. Nagot also wrote to a friend in 1803 that, during the first ten years, the apparent failure of the Seminary made him wish to return to France. See F. C. Nagot, Letter to C. M. Le Saulnier, Apr. 20, 1803, trans. L. Bruno (Baltimore: typed document in Nagot correspondence in the collection of the Associated Sulpicians of the U.S. at the AA).

11 Even in 1800 Carroll wrote to Plowden, "Gerogetown is not flourishing." See Ruane, 45.

12 For a readable and up-to-date history of the Maryland Jesuits, see Schroth.

13 There is something of a similarity here with the Sulpicians in Montreal. For a recent history of the Sulpician Province of Canada, see Dominique Deslandres, John A. Dickenson and Ollivier Hubert, *The Sulpicians of Montreal: A History of Power and Discretion, 1657-2007*, trans. Steven Watt (Montreal: Wilson and LeFleur, 2013).

Since the Catholic Church was not legally established in Maryland, the colonial government did not subsidize the Church. So the Jesuits had to accept land grants as a way to fund their ministry. They were also required to hold this property as individuals and not as a community.

After the Glorious Revolution, the Jesuits were double-taxed by the English government because they were considered Jacobite sympathizers.[14] These measures were augmented during the French and Indian War.[15] Nevertheless, in 1763, it was reported to the Holy See that the Jesuits owned five large estates totaling more than 12,000 acres. These holdings included a farm in northeastern part of Cecil County called Bohemia Manor.[16] That had been the site of a short-lived Jesuit school where John Carroll received his secondary education, before moving to Saint Omer's.[17]

The Jesuits of Maryland were never numerous. From 1634 to 1773, a total of 113 priests and 30 brothers had served in Maryland. At the time of their worldwide suppression in 1773, there were 25 Jesuit priests in the colonies,[18] and at the beginning of the American Revolution, only 20 remained.[19] Nevertheless, "this handful of Jesuits were, for all practical purposes, the roots and trunk of the colonial Catholic Church."[20] They were also the custodians of most of its financial resources.

The suppression of the Jesuits did not change the fact that under civil law the property of the former Jesuits was private property. So, looking toward the future, in 1783-1784 Carroll spearheaded the development of a new legal structure that would maintain this property for the support of the Church in the U.S.[21] Under this arrangement, the property was to be controlled by a committee called the Select Body of the Clergy, initially composed of five former Jesuits.[22]

At about the same time, Carroll wrote to Plowden, "The object nearest to my

---

14 See Ch. V., n. 44, above.

15 J. Fairfax McLauglin, *College Days at Georgetown and Other Papers* (Philadelphia: J. B. Lippincott, 1899), 42-43.

16 Spalding, *The Premier See*, 6. Curran wrote that there were seven estates totaling 12,677 acres. See Curran, *Bicentennial History*, I, 9.

17 Ibid., 6. See also Daley, 5.

18 See Schroth, 27.

19 Henry de Courcy, *The Catholic Church in the United States: Pages of Its History*. 2nd ed. (New York: Edward Dunnigan & Son, 1857), 37.

20 Ibid.

21 The State of Maryland approved the new structure in 1792.

22 Curran, *The Bicentennial History*, I, 11. Spalding points out that later, as bishop, Carroll had no special role in this Corporation. Rather the Corporation agreed to pay him an annual salary. This was in tune with Carroll's early desire not to become entangled in financial matters. Spalding, *The Premier See*, 25.

heart is to establish a college on this continent for the education of youth, which might at the same time become a Seminary for future Clergymen."[23] The following year, Carroll was appointed apostolic prefect for the U.S., and in 1785, he began to think about concrete options for the training of priests.[24] During the following year, The Select Body agreed to devote some income from their farms to the realization of Carroll's dream, and so Carroll then drew up a plan for a college, or academy, at Georgetown and obtained approval from the Holy See. He also had to defeat the objections of some of his former-Jesuit brothers who wanted to conserve all the financial resources for what they hoped would be the eventual reestablishment of the Society of Jesus.

Carroll's next problem was a lack of personnel, specifically a lack of priests, to staff the new academy in Georgetown. So his plan was that the faculty would consist entirely of lay teachers at first, until some priests would become available. It was only at the last minute that Carroll was able to find a priest to be president of the new institution. Moreover, since there was so little money available to him for faculty salaries, Carroll hoped that some courses could be taught less expensively by seminarians, if there were any.[25]

EARLY GEORGETOWN COLLEGE

23 Hanley, I, 78.
24 Curran, *The Bicentennial History*, I, 11ff.
25 Ibid., 32.

In Georgetown's early years, Nagot, at Carroll's request, sent several of his precious seminarians there to teach. Mondésir was the first – and the first resident faculty member at Georgetown – and he was followed by four others. Most did not return to the Seminary. Moreover, some Sulpicians were assigned to the faculty and administration of Georgetown.

In those early years, all hope was placed in Georgetown. However, relations with Georgetown only remained good for a short time. DuBourg arrived in Baltimore from his exile in Spain in December of 1794 and soon joined the Sulpicians. In the fall of 1796 Carroll appointed him, at the age of 30, as the third president of Georgetown. Carroll probably made this appointment at the recommendation of Nagot who knew DuBourg well. However, DuBourg's leadership of Georgetown met opposition from the trustees of the institution, especially those who were former Jesuits. So, in the middle of his third year in office, DuBourg resigned the post. One prominent historian put it diplomatically: "Rev. Mr. Du Bourg, as president, was, by his energy and activity, in advance of the trustees of that day, who had much of the deliberate, conservative ways of England, and could scarcely be brought to approve the enterprising spirit and popular ideas of the French priest."[26] In a blunter way, Carroll wrote to Plowden:

> In this untoward business, it is not easy to say, where the fault lies; most probably some on both sides. But national attachments, that bane of all communities where they are suffered to exist, have been the original cause of the business.[27]

To understand fully Carroll's suspicion about anti-French sentiment at the time, it is helpful to know that American attitudes toward France changed during the 1790s. Early in the decade, as we saw, most Americans strongly supported the French Revolution and saw it as part of the bigger struggle for liberty that also inspired the American Revolution. Although some were shocked by the September massacres in 1792 and by the execution of Louis XVI in January 1793, at that time there was still considerable support in the U.S. for France, especially in the south.[28]

However, military developments gradually undermined the harmony between the two countries. When wars broke out in 1793 between revolutionary France and other major European powers, President Washington declared the U.S. neutral, although "this was a clear violation of the U.S. treaty with France [in

---

26 John Gilmary Shea, *Memorial of the First Centenary of Georgetown College, D.C. Comprising a History of Georgetown University* (Washington: P.F. Collier, 1891), 23-24.

27 Ruane, 100.

28 Furstenberg, 41-42.

1778]."[29] Moreover, the French Revolution had spurred slave revolts in the French colony of Saint Domingue (Haiti), and the President's action blocked the French effort to get U.S. naval support against Great Britain in order to insure that France remained in control of that valuable colony.[30]

A SLAVE REVOLT IN SAINT DOMINGUE

At about this time, Washington began to see increasingly aggressive British military actions as a new threat to U.S. independence. And so in 1796 Washington concluded an agreement with Great Britain on some of the issues left over from the American Revolution. This further upset France and led it to break diplomatic ties with the U.S. Then the French navy began to seize American ships suspected of carrying British goods. This soured most Americans on France.

In 1797, while DuBourg was serving as president of Georgetown, the new U.S. President John Adams, hoping to avoid all-out war with France, sent

29 Ibid., 47.
30 The chaos in Saint Domingue caused a mass exodus from the island. It is said that the Catholic population of Philadelphia doubled as a result of these refugees. See Furstenberg, 109. A French-speaking black and creole Catholic community also appeared in Baltimore and settled around the new seminary. The exodus also seems to have doubled the number of Catholics in that city. Ibid., 107.

a delegation to France to try to resolve the conflict. When the delegation arrived in Paris, however, Talleyrand, France's new foreign minister under the relatively moderate government called the Directory, set onerous and offensive preconditions for talks. He even demanded a "substantial bribe."[31] This became known as the XYZ Affair. "When the country learned of the humiliations of the XYZ Affair in April of 1798, it went wild with anger against the French."[32] As a result, three months later Congress passed "The Aliens and Sedition Act," an anti-immigrant bill that led to the return of some French refugees to France and to Haiti.[33]

BRITISH CARTOON OF THE XYZ AFFAIR

So it was quite reasonable for Carroll to have suspected that DuBourg's presidency of Georgetown was to a considerable extent a casualty of the animosity caused by world events in 1798. There was also clearly a fear on the part of some former Jesuits that the Sulpicians wanted to take over control of their College.[34] Whatever the cause, the situation created ongoing tension, despite peacemaking efforts on Nagot's part. For example, at Carroll's request, he sent Maréchal to Georgetown in 1800 to teach philosophy. In December of that year, he and the rector of Saint Peter's were the principal assistants to Carroll at the episcopal

31 See Gordon S. Wood, *Empire of Liberty: A History of the Early Republic, 1789-1815* (Oxford, UK: Oxford University, 2009), 632 (of the Kindle edition).

32 Ibid., 635.

33 The XYZ Affair also contributed to the defeat of Adams in the 1800 election because, during the campaign, he came out in favor of reconciliation with France. Fortunately for the early Sulpicians in Baltimore, "the accommodation of French settlers and exiles did not depend on Maryland's acceptance and support of France." Gregory Wood, *The French Presence*, 147.

34 Ibid., 86 and Kauffman, 46. At this point, only the Sulpicians had qualified priests to teach there.

consecration of Leonard Neale, who was then the president of Georgetown.[35] A decade later, on June 18, 1809, Nagot would write down for posterity some reflections about the tension with the Jesuits. Among his thoughts, he wrote that he was "far from fearing the return of the Society of Jesus."[36] Rather, since he was a product of ten years of Jesuit education, he looked forward to their return as a child awaits the return of its mother after she has been away. Given this sentiment on his part, it must have been particularly uncomfortable for him to bear the distrust of some of the former Jesuits.

Financial Difficulties

When Nagot was leaving France for the U.S., Emery had advised him to invest in land when he got to Baltimore.[37] So, on September 24, 1792, Nagot used some of the remaining original money to purchase about ten additional acres near the seminary property.[38] According to Tessier, he also entered into a lease-purchase agreement for additional acreage in the area.[39] This property would become the core of what is known today as the Seton Hill Neighborhood in Baltimore. Entries in Tessier's diary, or journal, show that Nagot devoted time to leasing and developing this property during the first decade, and so he must have hoped that these investments would eventually provide a significant and stable source of income for the Seminary.

Nevertheless, in one instance at least, Nagot's efforts at property development led to a serious financial loss. He had to go to court more than once in the 1790s to address a legal complaint against the Seminary. It seems that a builder hired by the Sulpicians ran away with a payment they had given him but he left his workers unpaid. Unfortunately, the Sulpician treasurer at the time, Father Chicoisneau,[40] indicated to the workers that he would see that they got what they were owed. This created a financial liability for the Sulpicians, and they did not have the funds to discharge it. Nagot noted that Americans were a litigious people and he commented as follows on the costly outcome of the trial,

---

35 See Sr. M. Bernetta Brislen, "The Episcopacy of Leonard Neale, Second Archbishop of Baltimore," in *Historical Records and Studies*, XXXIV (New York: The U.S. Catholic Historical Society,1945), 35.

36 F. C.Nagot, "Memorial Which I Began to Write in 1809 to Be Read After My Death", June 18, 1809 (Baltimore: Nagot personal papers in the collection of the Associated Sulpicians of the U.S. at the AA).

37 Emery, "Counsels," section 15. The endowment of Catholic institutions in France was usually in the form of land that could be worked or leased for income, and the land of the Maryland Jesuits was their main source of income during the colonial period.

38 Tessier, *Epoques*, 2. Tessier indicates later that this property extended eastward to present-day Eutaw Street. See Ibid. 13.

39 Ibid., 2.

40 Chicoisneau became treasurer in 1792. He was replaced by Tessier in 1796.

Ita pater quoniam sic fuit placitum ante te. A good lesson for the future. One will not see me in court again. It would be necessary to drag me there.[41]

In the context of Nagot's financial challenges, it might also be noted that the early Sulpicians in Baltimore owned slaves.[42] It seems that they first purchased some toward the end of 1793 when they were trying to respond to the "distressing condition" of their finances.[43] On August 20, in the context of a discussion about the need to reduce the domestic staff,

> Someone said that it was scarcely possible, in this country, to find good domestics who would be stable and become attached to the house. So the surest way would be to try to get black domestics, the best we could acquire, because slaves do not have the freedom of seeking work elsewhere.[44]

On another occasion, Tessier, then the Seminary's treasurer, noted in his diary that he and Nagot went out together to see if they could purchase a slave. Tessier also recorded that he rented slaves from their owners for particular tasks.[45]

How should this be evaluated? First, in this as in other matters, Nagot was a man of his times. The Church had condemned the abuses of slavery, but not the insitution as such,[46] and, as we saw earlier, Nagot's early years were spent in and near Nantes, the center of the French slave trade. Moreover, with respect to slavery, Maryland was a southern state. In 1790 about one-third of Maryland's population consisted of slaves. Many well-to-do Maryland farmers used them to work the land. The Jesuits had hundreds of slaves working on their plantations in the early 19th century.[47] By the time Nagot came to Maryland, though few

---

41 F. C. Nagot, Letter to Le Saulnier, n.d. (spring, 1798), trans. L. Bruno (Baltimore: typed document in Nagot Correspondence in the Collection of the Associated Sulpicians of the U.S. at the AA). Though this letter is not dated, Nagot mentions in it that he had just received the news that French General Louis-Alexandre Berthier had invaded Rome and arrested Pope Pius VI. This happened on Feb. 10, 1798. Nagot's response to this outrage was: "I've lost sleep this night and I carry within me everywhere the thought of the Church's misfortunes. We don't know what has become of the Holy Father....Our Lord will sustain his Church. That should console us and keep us steadfast in our faith." Ibid.

42 It is unclear how many, but the number was probably very small due to the limited needs of the Sulpicians in Baltimore. A source of confusion about this is the fact that Tessier sometimes used "our Negro" to denote a person on the payroll, not a slave. See, e.g., Tessier, Historical diary, 9-35.

43 Minutes of the Faculty Meetings of the Baltimore Seminary, trans. R. MacDonough. (Baltimore: typed translation in AA), Aug. 14, 1793.

44 Ibid.

45 Tessier, "Historical diary", 1-10. See especially the entry for Dec. 10, 1796

46 Only specific practices related to enslavement and to the slave trade had been explicitly condemned. See Robert E. Curran, "Rome, the American Church and Slavery," in *Building the Church in America*, eds. J. Linck and R. Kupke (Washington: The Catholic University, 1999), 33.

47 See ibid. See also Curran, "'Splendid Poverty:' Jesuit Slaveholding in Maryland, 1805-1838," in *Catholics in the Old South*, eds. R. Miller and J. Wakelyn (Macon, GA: Mercer University, 1983), 125-146.

slaves were being imported from Africa or the Caribbean, there were still many slave traders operating in Baltimore.

For a half-century before the Civil War, more than a dozen slave traders operated from harborside storefronts along Pratt and adjacent streets. Some advertised regularly in The Sun and other papers, declaring "5,000 Negroes Wanted" or "Negroes! Negroes! Negroes!" In an 1845 city directory, "Slave Dealers" are listed between "Silversmiths" and "Soap."[48]

FOR SALE,
A Healthy Negro Woman,
About 19 years of age ; she is smart, capable of all kinds of Housework and is an excellent Cook. For terms apply to the subscriber near Pratt street Bridge.
SALIADORE LOWRIE.

He has also TWO PLEASURE BOATS, for the accommodation of those gentlemen who are fond of this most agreeable diversion, which can be had at any time at the lower end of Dugan's wharf, at a moderate price.
july 13   d4t*

ADVERTISEMENT FOR THE SALE OF A SLAVE AND TWO BOATS IN BALTIMORE, 1814
(MARYLAND HISTORICAL ARCHIVES)

The fact remains that Nagot and the early Sulpicians left no evidence of moral reservations about the practice of slavery, despite its inherently degrading nature.[49]

---

48 Scott Shane, "The Secret History of City Slave Trade," at http://articles.baltimoresun.com/1999-06-20/topic/9906220293_1_slave-trade-buy-slaves-slaves-were-sold (accessed 1/11/16).

49 There was already an abolitionist society in Baltimore at the time, and it is interesting to note that Thayer caused consternation in more than one of his assignments due to his opposition to slavery. See, e.g., Hanley, II, 122-123. Carroll himself was not an abolitionist, but he favored gradual emancipation. See Curran, "Rome," 35-38.

It appears that the early Sulpicians bought slaves because, despite the real estate investments made by Nagot in the early years, the lack of seminarians created financial difficulties for them after only two years. In 1793, as the original funds began to run out, Nagot knew that the Sulpicians in France were not in a position to help.[50] So he first turned to the Canadian Sulpicians who were not numerous at the time but who did have some financial resources.[51] They gave a generous donation that was augmented by a personal gift from Nagot's friend Delavau.[52]

THE *BOURSE* OF FATHER NAGOT

Then Nagot turned to Carroll who, in 1790, had expressed to him and to Emery the hope that he could find a way to assist financially after the first two years.[53] So in 1793 Carroll appealed to The Select Body, and they gave the Sulpicians the use of Bohemia Manor under a contract negotiated by Nagot. He took possession of the farm on May 13, 1793, but, for various reasons, the farm never provided much revenue for the Seminary.

---

50 See Hanley, II, 79.

51 When the British took over Canada, those twenty-eight Sulpicians who were willing to transfer their allegiance to Britain were able to retain their property. However, they were not permitted to import any more Sulpicians from France. Thus, in 1792, there were only nine Canadian Sulpicians. See Molac, 74.

52 Ruane, 68. Nagot wrote to Monteal in 1795 and in 1798 for more help. See Minutes of the Faculty Meeting, September 2, 1795. See also F. C. Nagot, Letter to Le Saulnier, n.d. It seems that they received some additional help.

53 Hanley, I, 462 and 516. In 1791 Carroll had already helped them obtain the gift of a small farm that they sold. See Minutes of the Faculty Meeting, Sept. 12 & 19, 1791.

So there was no good solution to the early financial difficulties of the Seminary. In May of 1776, Nagot wrote to a friend:

> We are in extreme need, in debt to many. We are at the brink of borrowing. If we consider borrowing, we will borrow more than we owe. The concern about paying debts owed makes me sad and sometimes I lose sleep. I have never seen myself in such a crisis. Blessed be God! I have begun, for the second time today, a novena to the Blessed Virgin to obtain for me what is necessary to save me from this painful and disturbing situation.[54]

While the poverty of his community created worries for Nagot during this period, on a personal level Nagot embraced poverty and the simple life. For example, in 1794, with some assistance from Tessier, he used his own personal funds to donate a piece of property to the Seminary.[55] Two years later, he made a private vow of poverty.[56]

While not asking everyone to take such a vow, in November, 1797 Nagot urged his confreres to maintain a simple lifestyle:

> The Superior remarked how proper it is for us to stick to the old frugality at meals, just as it exists in France in all our seminaries, especially since at the present time most of our dear confreres, dispersed on all sides, led a life full of suffering and affliction, while we live in peace here, and, so to speak, in abundance.[57]

As financial difficulties persisted, in March 1798, while DuBourg was at Georgetown, rumors arose in the diocese that the Sulpicians "are becoming rich through Bohemia."[58] On August 30, 1799, shortly after DuBourg's departure from Georgetown and just as Bohemia Manor was actually about to become more productive, some prominent members of The Select Body demanded that the Sulpicians return the farm to them so that they could use it to support

---

54 F. C. Nagot, Letter to Anonymous [Le Saulnier?], May 1, 1796, trans. L. Bruno (Baltimore: typed document in Nagot Correspondence in the Collection of the Associated Sulpicians of the U.S. at the AA).

55 Minutes of the Faculty Meeting, Dec. 19, 1794.

56 See F. C. Nagot, "*Mon Testament Spirituel*" (Baltimore: handwritten document in Nagot correspondence in the Collection of the Associated Sulpicians of the U.S. at the AA, 1809), 6. In this document he declared that he owned nothing. He reaffirmed this Testament in 1812.

57 Minutes of the Faculty Meeting, Nov. 21, 1797. However, the minutes indicate that one confrere objected, saying that the U.S. was a different place from France.

58 Minutes of the Faculty Meeting, Mar. 2, 1798.

Georgetown.[59] The Sulpicians complied willingly despite the severe financial setback that this demand entailed, and Nagot tried to smooth things over in a conciliatory letter of August 22, 1799. "We are not displeased," he wrote, "that today this passes to the clergy; it is a proof which we offer of the respectful deference which I have the honor to be [*sic*] in the name of my confreres."[60]

The Founding of Saint Mary's College

At about this time, Nagot's hope that Georgetown would be a good source of seminarians was fading. However, a new possibility arose. He learned from Emery that a young Sulpician named Pierre Babad (1763-1846) had received permission to go from exile in Spain to ministry in the U.S. Emery explained that, on his way to Baltimore, Babad had stopped in Cuba and quickly became very confident that he would be able to open an ecclesiastical college for the Archdiocese of Havana. In support of this proposal, Emery extended Nagot's mandate to cover any Sulpician enterprise that might take root in Cuba.

So on October 9, 1798, Nagot wrote to Babad that he would be very relieved if Babad "could send some men to the seminary, since Georgetown did not promise much."[61] Then a few months later, Nagot sent DuBourg to assess the situation. He had already pulled Flaget out of Georgetown and sent him to Cuba as well. When it became clear that Babad's initiative would not bear fruit, DuBourg tried to establish a school in another part of Cuba. In the end, these efforts came to nothing because of resistance to the presence of French Sulpicians on the part of the local clergy and the local Spanish colonial authorities.[62]

On August 9, 1799, while Nagot was negotiating the terms of the withdrawal of the Sulpicians from Bohemia Manor,[63] DuBourg returned to Baltimore, bringing with him several Spanish-speaking Cuban students. He proposed to Nagot the establishment of an academy in Baltimore. "Father Nagot sincerely believed that this new institution would provide at least some candidates for the seminary."[64] Perhaps it would become the feeder insititution he needed.

---

59 The enrollment at Georgetown declined under DuBourg's successors. There were only 20 students there in 1803. There was fear at that time that the institution might fail. See Daley, 112-113.

60 Ibid., 93. According to the contract that Nagot had negotiated, The Select Body had the right reclaim the use of the property at any time.

61 Melville, 75. See also F. C. Nagot, Transcript of Letter to Babad, Oct. 9, 1793 (Baltimore: Nagot correspondence in the collection fo the Associated Sulpicians of the U.S. at the AA).

62 Kauffman, 48. Kauffman explains that the Cuba ventures failed because the influence of Jansenism was strong among the Cuban clergy at the time and because the Spanish colonial government feared the influence of "liberal" Frenchmen. So again, European politics affected the Sulpicians in the U.S. Also, Babad's lack of tact contributed to the failure of the Cuba venture. See Ruane, 101-103.

63 Wisely, Nagot would not relinquish Bohemia Manor until he had a letter of financial release from The Select Body.

64 Ruane, 96. See also Faillon, 77.

Everyone expected that it would, at the very least, produce excess income that would assist with the cost of priestly formation.[65] The new school, called St. Mary's College, opened two months later. It soon became known as "DuBourg's college."

Not surprisingly, the establishment of the College further provoked the former Jesuits at Georgetown because they saw it as a direct competitor with their institution.[66] The fact that DuBourg was leading the new venture in Baltimore did not help. When Nagot took this matter to Carroll, Carroll must have been concerned because Nagot suggested to him that he set a limit on enrollment at the College.[67] In the spring of 1800, Nagot did further damage control by meeting with Carroll and Neale, then the president of Georgetown who was about to become Carroll's coadjutor bishop. Nagot told them that St. Mary's College would limit its enrollment in two ways: it would admit only foreigners – apparently he meant primarily Spanish-speaking Cubans and French-speakers from the Caribbean[68] – and it would hold enrollment at a maximum of 25. Moreover, the College would give free education to any students who came to the seminary from Georgetown and did not have the means to pay.[69]

Despite these restraints, the former Jesuits at Georgetown soon made a decision that hurt the Seminary. Still short of student-teachers, they kept seven students at Georgetown for the study of philosophy who wished to prepare for the priesthood.[70] Carroll had not approved this decision in advance and was not comfortable with it because he recognized that he had the right to make decisions that affected the preparation of those pursuing priesthood. Nevertheless, he did not block this move and he again attributed it to anti-French prejudice.[71]

Some historians have given the impression that St. Mary's College was almost entirely DuBourg's doing. However, it is important to recall that Nagot had established "Monsieur DuBourg's House" in Issy. In a similar way, the older

---

65 Minutes of the Faculty Meeting, Sept. 20, 1799.

66 See Daley, 107-108.

67 Hanley, 314. See also Tessier *Epoques*, 9. In 1800, for financial reasons, Nagot proposed to his confreres that the enrollment be increased to 24 or 25, knowing that Carroll would not object. See Minutes of the Faculty Meeting, Apr. 11, 1800.

68 Curran has pointed out that the restriction of enrollment to students from the Caribbean (i.e., French and Spanish-speaking students) did not comfort the leadership at Georgetown because a number of Georgetown's early students were from the West Indies. Curran, *The Bicentennial History*, I, 55

69 Kauffman, 48. There is a reference to the Spanish-speaking students learning French with the aid of the French-speaking ones.

70 Ibid., 49. Nagot had no more seminarians to send there to teach, and the former Jesuits planned that these philosophy students would teach the younger students at Georgetown for a modest salary. These prospective seminarians were bound by an oath to stay at Georgetown. See Curran, *The Bicentennial History*, I, 54.

71 According to Spalding, Carroll gradually became more partial toward the Sulpicians than toward his former Jesuit brothers. See Spalding, *The Premier See*, 19.

and more experienced local superior in Baltimore played an active role in the establishment of "DuBourg's college" in Baltimore. Nagot saw this move as legitimate because, in Emery's initial instructions, he had written that the Sulpicians could take charge of a college.[72] Moreover, letters from Emery to Nagot during the 1790s showed that Emery continued to believe very strongly that the U.S. needed more Catholic colleges or academies that might be feeders for the Seminary and that these might have to be established by Sulpicians for the sake of the Seminary's survival.[73] For these reasons Nagot first tried to support Georgetown and then, when Georgetown produced few seminarians, he took an interest in the possibility of a Sulpician college or academy in Cuba. When that venture came to nothing, and with a Seminary enrollment of only one in 1799 and two in 1800, it would have been natural for Nagot to work closely with DuBourg to found St. Mary's College in Baltimore.[74] Though DuBourg was not proposing to open a minor seminary properly speaking, we have seen that Nagot clearly hoped that DuBourg's enterprise would help to prepare some students to enter the Seminary,[75] and even if that did not happen, it might provide some income to keep the seminary going.[76]

Carroll, though not initially in favor of St. Mary's College, did not prohibit it. In January, 1801, he wrote, "Father Nagot, whose virtue and merit of every kind I revere, was zealous for the execution of this project, and has not ceased to represent the usefulness which it would afford to my diocese."[77] At one point, Nagot even appealed to the American love of liberty to win Carroll over.[78]

In light of all this, it is only fair to say that Nagot was the founder of St. Mary's College at least as much as was DuBourg. Ten years later, Nagot sounded anything but passive when, in retrospect, he noted that in founding the College he did not violate his obligation of obedience because neither Carroll nor Emery had forbidden its opening or ordered him to close it down. Then he added:

> The college…was up to us then, who had our finger upon the necessity, it was up to us to prosecute what was needful for the undertaking of the seminary, and consequently the formation of a college under pain of otherwise abandoning the place and

---

72 Emery, "Counsels," para. 6. Emery believed that most of the students there would go on to ordination.

73 See *"Extraits de différentes lettres de M'. Emery, faits par M'. Nagot,"* Ruane, 112. Emery's later reluctance to endorse St. Mary's College, as we shall see, was partly motivated by Carroll's concern to avoid conflict with Georgetown.

74 This interpretation follows Melville's on page 83 of her biography of DuBourg.

75 Faillon, *Histoire*, I, 77-78.

76 Ruane, 96.

77 Ibid., 107. For a specific example of Nagot's advocacy on behalf of the opening of the college, see his letter to Carroll of August 26, 1800, at ibid., 106.

78 Ibid.

recrossing the sea – which we infallibly would have done if we continued to be unemployed in this diocese as we had been for about ten years.[79]

At any rate, at the end of the Sulpicians' first ten years in the U.S., the ongoing conflict with the former Jesuits at Georgetown and lack of enthusiasm about the College on the part of Carroll and Emery were matters of such serious concern that Nagot and his confreres seriously considered moving the college to a distant location[80] or even closing it in favor of Georgetown.[81]

Emery and Developments in France

As the 1790s progressed, Emery became another source of worry for Nagot and they corresponded often.[82] Nagot and the others were clearly happy not to be in France.[83] But they were also anxious for any news of their native land, and most of the news that came from Emery was upsetting. In August and September of 1792 the French Revolution lurched to the left.[84] On August 18, the Society of Saint Sulpice was formally suppressed. Just before that, as Imperial and Prussian armies under the command of the Duke of Brunswick[85] moved toward Paris, a mob broke into the Tuileries Palace, and Louis XVI and Marie Antoinette were arrested. Fearful of counter-revolution, the revolutionary leadership began to arrest anyone else who might turn against them, including non-juring priests. Radicals like Marat urged that they be killed.

A series of massacres then took place during the first two weeks of September, beginning on September 2 with the killing of two-hundred bishops and priests held at the Carmes, including the eight Blessed Sulpician Martyrs.[86] That month, the National Convention, a new and more extreme government, came to power. Fortunately for the new government, on September 20, a French force repulsed Brunswick at Valmy.

---

79 Ruane, 96. Ruane, however, interprets this text as saying that Nagot "consented" to the opening of the college primarily in order to bring the Sulpicians in the U.S. back together in Baltimore – most of them were in the missions – and so to preserve them for priestly formation in the U.S. This interpretation seems to be putting the cart before the horse and does not agree with Emery's support for the opening of colleges in other places. That is, for Nagot, the primary reason for St. Mary's College was to provide a feeder for the seminary.

80 Ibid., 50 and especially 115. See also Hanley II, 332-333.

81 Curran, *The Bicentennial History*, I, 55.

82 Only a few of their letters or parts of their letters have survived, but they are enough to show that Nagot kept Emery apprised of major developments, and vice versa.

83 See, e.g., Hanley, II, 22.

84 Some historians speak of a second French Revolution at this time.

85 He was Carl Wilhelm Ferdinand, Prince-Duke of Brunschweig-Wolfenbüttel (1735-1806) and, before the invasion of France, he issued the Brunswick Manifesto designed to intimidate the French population.

86 "The Carmes" was a Carmelite monastery (*monastère des Carmes*) that was converted into a prison during the French Revolution.

MASSACRE AT THE CARMES (BNF)

At this time, Emery was able to avoid imprisonment. He quickly shut down the remaining Sulpician programs in Paris, but he decided to continue living at the Seminary with a few confrères where he continued to carry out his duties as a vicar general of Paris. This activity, however, soon led to his arrest on May 19, 1793, when one of his letters to the archbishop of Paris in exile was intercepted by agents of the government and was deemed counter-revolutionary. The government also tried to use another letter against him, one that he had written to Edgemont and that spoke about funds that he had sent with Nagot to Baltimore.[87] On May 31, from his cell, Emery wrote in a letter to Villèle, now in exile in Germany, that he feared that he and his fellow prisoners would be

---

87 The investigators thought that the money went to Baltimore in British Ireland.

victims of another September massacre but that he was prepared to die.[88]

This is the context for a moving letter of Emery to Nagot, dated April 28, 1793.[89] Convinced that he was about to be sent to the guillotine, he explained to Nagot that one of the charges against him was that he had sent funds along with Nagot to Baltimore.[90] Then he wrote, "What a consolation to die the victim of my love for the Church and of my affection for you." He went on to share some of his final thoughts. Among them was a reminder that Nagot was responsible for Sulpician endeavors in the U.S. Then he added: "I need not ask you to love all your confreres as a father loves his children." Since it took at least three months for mail to cross the Atlantic, Nagot must have received this letter in late May not knowing whether Emery was alive or dead. However, Emery escaped execution and was released in October.

Nevertheless, on July 16 he was rearrested and on August 3 he was transferred from the Carmes to the forbidding Conciergerie, a prison that earned the name, "the antechamber to the guillotine." There he would remain for eight months while being interrogated by agents the notorious Committee for Public Safety. Imprisoned there with Emery were Louis XVI and Marie Antoinette.[91] On April 4, 1794, Emery was transferred to the Collège de Plessis, an improvised prison, where his trial came to a climax. In the end, he was acquitted and returned to live at the Seminary.

During the next few years, Emery was called upon several times to give his opinion on the various loyalty oaths that the National Convention (and, later, the Directory) imposed on priests who did not take the oath to support the Civil Constitution. This required him to use his considerable expertise as a canon lawyer and moral theologian. His opinions were very influential, and some of them caused controversy among the clergy. Nagot wrote to him in the mid-1790s, objecting strongly to the stance he took on one of the oaths.[92] This shows that Nagot was willing to disagree with his superior on an important matter.

Toward the end of the decade, during the rise of Napoleon, Emery's

---

88 Gosselin, I, 357.

89 See Ruane, 18-20. Ruane also reports on page 20 that, on the same day, Emery wrote to another confrere: "I die in the hope and consolation that the name and spirit of Saint Sulpice will not wholly perish. Maryland will preserve them." See also Méric, *Histoire*, 310.

90 See note 87, above.

91 Louis was executed while Emery was at the Conciergerie. Emery ministered to Marie Antoinette. One of her recent biographers Desmond Seward called Emery the prison's "unofficial chaplain." For details, see, e.g., H. I. D. Ryder, "M. Emery, Superior of Saint Sulpice, 1789-1811," *The Dublin Review*, Third Series, 18 (July-Oct. 1887), 256. See also Méric, *Histoire*, 315ff.

92 Gosselin, I, 409. Gosselin described Nagot's communication as *"une lettre très-forte."* Apparently, this letter no longer exists.

THE CONCIERGERIE, 1790

communications raised new questions for Nagot: Emery was beginning to contemplate recalling Sulpicians to France. This change in Emery's thinking needs some context. From 1796 until 1798 Napoleon served as a successful and increasingly popular general under the penultimate revolutionary government known as the Directory. Sensing the shift in the wind, Talleyrand was one of those who wrote to him, urging him to enter politics. In the fall of 1799, just as France was facing the danger of another foreign invasion, Napoleon returned to Paris, overthrew the Directory, and established a Consulate in which he served as one of the three consuls. Shortly afterwards, he staged a kind of coup within a coup and had himself declared First Consul on December 12, 1799.

The Consulate brought stability to France, and it was evident to Emery that

NAPOLEON AS FIRST CONSUL

Napoleon wanted to address the broken condition of the Church in order to resolve a long-standing source of civil division and strife. This he did in negotiations with the Holy See that led to a Condordat, signed in 1802. The following year, Chateaubriand's trend-setting *Genius of Christianity* was published in France. In it he criticized the philosophes for their failure to appreciate the beauty and power of religion.[93] Napoleon promoted this book as a kind of argument for the Concordat.

This dramatic shift in the political and cultural climate in France encouraged Emery to move toward the restoration of the Society in France and the reopening of seminaries there. He concluded that he would have to recall some or all the Sulpicians in exile, including those in the U.S., especially since the Seminary in Baltimore had amost no students and since many of the Sulpicians in the U.S. were not engaged in priestly formation. Carroll begged him not to terminate the seminary and not to deprive the U.S. of some of its most capable priests, but Emery was primarily concerned about the need to rebuild the Church in France.

At that time, Nagot also had to contend with Emery's serious reservations about the College. Emery's main concern was that Carroll was not comfortable with it and had been pressured into accepting it. Emery also had serious reservations about DuBourg's priorities. Though our knowledge of these things comes mostly from letters that Emery wrote to Carroll and to DuBourg, Emery also communicated his concerns to Nagot.[94] Moreover, it is likely that, with the growing need for Sulpicians to return to France, Emery could not see the point of supporting a college that was not a minor seminary. At this point, Nagot knew that his ten years of labor in Baltimore might come to nothing.

---

93 Apparently, by this time, Chateaubriand no longer embraced the enlightened views that Nagot found suspect during their voyage to the U.S. in 1791.

94 See, for example, F. C. Nagot, Letter to C. M. Le Saulnier, Apr. 20, 1803, trans. L. Bruno (Baltimore: typed document in Nagot correspondence in the collection of the Associated Sulpicians of the U.S. at the AA), 1. In this letter, Nagot told Le Saulnier that Emery considered the admission of Protestants to be both complex and bold ("*une chose délicate et hardie*"). Nevertheless, Nagot felt that Emery did not fully appreciate what was at stake when this decision was made. "In France…one cannot see us and thus understand what is happening here."

Health Problems

Low enrollment at the seminary, tension with former Jesuits, and coping with Emery's decision to end, or at least curtail, the Sulpician mission in the U.S. were not the only burdens that Nagot had to bear during his first decade in the U.S. Never a robust man, Nagot suffered two life-threatening illnesses during that period. We know that the first was in 1795, and the second in 1796.

Regarding the first, Tessier wrote:

> On the 22nd or 25th of March, the Superior, being at dinner at the bishop's house, was struck as with an attack of apoplexy; they had to bring him back to the seminary in a coach; he was in great danger for several days, but the danger lessened gradually, though he never entirely recovered from the attack.[95]

A British medical textbook from the period defined apoplexy as follows:

> The term Apoplexia was employed by the Greeks, and is still used, to denote a disease in which the patient falls to the ground, often suddenly, and lies without sense or voluntary motion. Persons instantaneously thus affected, as if struck by lightning, were, by the ancients, denominated, attoniti [dazed], syderati.[96]

So Nagot, 61, had a stroke at Carroll's house. Since the cause of stroke was not known at that time, there was no effective treatment, and the prognosis was not encouraging. In Nagot's case, the stroke must not have been a major one because some rest seemed to revive him.[97] However, as Tessier added, the stroke left Nagot somewhat weaker than he had been beforehand.[98] This must have been the main reason that Nagot told his confreres in September, 1795 that he wished to resign as superior, but the minutes of that meeting state that everyone opposed him on this.[99]

On May 1, 1796, a little over a year after his stroke, Nagot sent a letter to an

---

95 Tessier, "Historical diary," 4.

96 Pandora Pound, et al. "From apoplexy to stroke," in *Age and Ageing*, 26 (1997), 331-332. Accessed on Dec. 8, 215 at http://ageing.oxfordjournals.org/content/26/5/331.full.pdf.

97 Tessier, *Epoques*, 4.

98 Five months after his stroke, Nagot lost Louis-Cesar Delavau, 53, his friend from Tours. Tessier wrote simply, "On the 20th of August, Delavau died suddenly after a slight indisposition which lasted two or three days." Ibid., 5.

99 Minutes of the Faculty Meeting, Sept. 2, 1795.

unidentified confrere in Canada.[100] In that letter he indicated that the effects of the stroke were still with him:

> I was seriously ill during the Lenten season last year. The illness was a harsh resounding blow which warned me to think of my last moment in a most serious way and which made me think of all the sins of my life which was soon coming to an end. I don't know what will result from it but since the last attack I find myself, body and soul, weakened. The least bit of exertion tires me to a great degree. Despite all that I can do, God only knows how much the nervous disorder, the terrible attack of illness, has been increasing considerably every day and has been throwing me into weariness and melancholy. Alas! All I can do is pray to God and delight in his presence in the retreat I provided for myself in my room making it a tomb for me. At any moment eternity which is only two steps away from me will come to me. The manner in which I do spiritual reading and a half hour of prayer, as simple as it might be, consisting of simple sentiments, wearies me, for I attend to every detail. I can do almost nothing else. O, God! The conversation of visitors is wearisome. It makes me sad. May God be pleased with the sacrifice I offer him every day of my poor life...***Fiat voluntas tua.*** I begin my days that way. I pray during the day and end my day in prayer. May death find in me the great love expressed in my poor prayers.[101]

Only a few months after these words were written, Nagot was afflicted with a second severe illness. Tessier described it as follows:

> On the fourth of July, Father Nagot caught an intermittent fever which became so violent that we feared for his life. The doctor stopped it with <u>quinouina</u> [sic] at the fourth attack.[102]

In his diary, under July 9, 1796, Tessier added, "The Superior took some tan (?) [sic] bark all day, to get rid of the fever; it worked."[103]

---

100 His addressee was probably the Sulpician Candide-Michel Le Saulnier. See below for more information about him.

101 F. C. Nagot, Letter to an anonymous friend. Trans. L. Bruno (Baltimore: Nagot correspondence in AA, May 1, 1796).

102 Ibid., 6. It is unclear why "quinouina" was underlined by the translator.

103 Jean Tessier, "Historical diary of the Treasurer of the Seminary of Baltimore," trans. J. Kortendick, section for 1796 and 1797, Part I (Baltimore: typed document in the Collection of the Associated Sulpicians of the U.S. at the AA), 1-3. The French word for the adjective "tan" is smudged in the original. That is why the translator put a question mark after it.

"Quinquina"[104] is the name of a tree that grows in the high Andes of Peru, where the native peoples ground up its bark and used the powder to treat fevers, among other things.[105] A more Eurocentric tradition is that quinquina was discovered in Peru in the 16th century by a Spanish Jesuit missionary. In any event, it was found to have a positive effect in treating malaria. So in the 17th century, quinquina was exported to Europe and used to treat the long-standing scourge of malaria there. At that time, it got the name "Jesuit bark,"[106] in French, *"poudre des Jésuites"*, or *"herbe des jésuites."*[107] So it is clear that that the bark that Nagot took was quinquina.

Jesuit Bark

It might seem strange to think that Nagot contracted malaria in the vicinity of Baltimore. However, malaria was introduced into the New World by European colonization, and, once introduced, it spread quickly. In the 18th century, the lowlands around the Chesapeake were home to malaria-bearing mosquitos in the summer. Moreover, until the end of the 19th century, malaria was considered a serious health threat in tidewater Maryland.[108]

Malaria is curable today if the patient is given a medication derived from quinine early enough during the first attack. Otherwise, since the malaria parasites remain alive in the body of the patient, the symptoms can recur from time to time in a more or less serious manner.

This second illness increased Nagot's desire to step down as superior. He shared this only with Garnier, and, in March, 1797 Garnier wrote to Emery: "I would much wish that Providence would send us some sharp and prudent confrere who could fill in for M. Nagot, who since his illness is no longer capable of

---

104 The English translation of Tessier spells the word "quinouina," but in the original French text the word is "quinquina," from which we get the word quinine. See Jean Tessier, *Epoques*, 7.

105 "Quinine," in *Dictionary of American Indian Contributions*, 221. Some call the tree the cinchona tree, and the bark only is called quinquina.

106 See, e.g., George W. Traub, *An Ignatian Spirituality Reader* (Chicago: Loyola Press, 2008), 14.

107 Quinine was only isolated from quinquina in 1820.

108 See, e.g., William T. Watson, M.D., "The Present Decline of Malaria in Maryland," in *Maryland Medical Journal*, XLVIII, no. 8 (August, 1905), 292. (289-302

dealing with matters and whom we fear with good reason will not last long."[109]

Nagot also wrote to Emery and asked for a replacement. Emery seemed willing to consider this at least and authorized Nagot to contact Father Candide-Michel Le Saulnier (1758-1830) in Montreal to find out if he would be willing to accept the appointment. Nagot wrote to Le Saulnier:

> I had written to him [Emery] upon recovering from the serious illnesses I had been enduring for two years in order to ask him to give me a successor. He answered me that his intention was that I be superior as long as I live, but the present state of my health does not allow me to expect a long life. Seeing that he authorizes me to urge you to come to Baltimore with the intention of replacing me. I beg you, my dear Father, in the name of our very reverend Father to take this important matter into consideration....Come, come practice charity toward a man who after having seen you as a Sulpician novice, will be filled with joy to have seen you as the head of the seminary in Baltimore, for you are the priest who is considered to be the best suited of all for this position.[110]

Le Saulnier had attended the seminary in Paris and was ordained a priest in 1782. He immediately joined the Sulpicians.[111] In 1792, he fled France for Britain where he was fortunate to obtain an official letter of introduction to the lieutenant-governor of Lower Canada. This enabled him to go there, reversing the longstanding British policy of not accepting French immigrant-priests. He was quickly appointed as the 15th pastor of Notre-Dame, the enormous Sulpician parish in Montreal, and he remained pastor there until 1821.

Le Saulnier replied to Nagot that he had to remain in Canada to assist the aged Canadian superior, Father Gabriel-Jean Brassier (1729-1798). Nagot accepted this: "*Eius manu sumus et non est voluntatis nostrae....Dominus providebit* [We are the works of His hands and and not of our own will....The Lord will provide.]."[112]

---

109 *"Je désirerais bien que la Providence nous envoyât quelque confrère éclairé et prudent qui pût suppléer au défaut de M. Nagot, qui depuis sa maladie n'est plus aussi capable d'affaires et que nous craignons avec fondement de ne pas conserver longtemps."* Méric, 141.

110 F. C. Nagot, Letter to Le Saulnier, July 16, 1797, trans. L. Bruno (Baltimore: Nagot correspondence in the Collection of the Associated Sulpicians of the U.S. at the AA).

111 For information on Le Saulnier, see Anonymous, "Le Saulnier, Candide-Michel," in *Dictionnaire biographique du Canada*, at http://www.biographi.ca/fr/bio/le_saulnier_candide_michel_6F.html (accessed Jan. 4, 2016).

112 F. C. Nagot, Letter to Le Saulnier, Sept. 18, 1797, trans. L. Bruno (Baltimore: typed document in Nagot correspondence in the Collection of the Associated Sulpicians of the U.S. at the AA), 1.

Fortunately, Nagot's health improved but not without some setbacks. For example, there is an entry in Tessier's diary in 1799 where he wrote that, throughout July and August of that year, Nagot was not well.[113] Yet, he bounced back in September. So, during the second half of the 1790s, Nagot had periods of serious illness but he still managed to lead the community as he was able.

Other Experiences

Not all that happened during Nagot's first ten years here was a burden for him. He did other things than struggle with severe administrative challenges and cope with health crises. First, he did some teaching at the seminary. For most of the 1790s, he taught dogmatic theology while Tessier taught moral theology and Garnier taught scripture. Since there were so few seminarians during that decade, much teaching was very likely in the form of tutoring.[114]

Second, like the other Sulpicians in Baltimore,[115] but to a lesser extent, he had a ministry outside the seminary. That ministry was mainly at Saint Peter's Pro-cathedral. Nagot had a very good voice,[116] and, as one of his duties, he led liturgical music there.[117] Mondésir described a painful but humorous episode that happened at Saint Peter's early in Nagot's time in Baltimore:

> Under the influence of his inspiration, which was altogether Catholic and Roman, our superior endeavored to introduce Gregorian music into the Churches of North America. I would not blame the holy man; but one may laugh at what happened when he made his first attempt.[118]

Mondésir went on to write that when Nagot, "a grave and dignified man," began to lead the community in chant, there was nothing but discord. The harder Nagot tried to pull the voices together, the worse the cacophony got. "There is danger" Mondésir wrote, "that the bishop, at his throne, will lose his gravity." [119] Mondésir ended his account with these words: "If our enthusiastic superior was humiliated, he took his humiliation well." And, in fact, he succeeded eventually

---

113 Jean Tessier, "Historical diary"," section for 1799, 4-5.

114 Ruane, 89.

115 Garnier, for example, was the first pastor of St. Patrick's in Fells Point, Baltimore's second parish, and returned to the leadership of that community after Floyd died. Tessier, the treasurer from 1792, was involved with ministry to Haitian refugees and later with the small community that met in the crypt of St. Mary's Chapel. Maréchal ran Bohemia Manor and later served at Georgetown.

116 Kauffman, 40.

117 Herbermann, 45.

118 Mondésir, "Souveniers, 1st installment, 22.

119 Mondésir added that Carroll, "a former Jesuit, had not much taste for chant." Ibid.

in teaching the congregation how to sing chant.[120]

This effort on Nagot's part was more significant than this story would seem to indicate. Back in 1790, Carroll had expressed the hope that the arrival of the Sulpicians would help him enhance worship at his cathedral,[121] and he got his wish. On April 23, 1792, he wrote to the Holy See:

> Since their [the Sulpicians'] arrival there has been notable improvement in conducting ecclesiastical functions and in the celebration of divine worship. To such a degree is this the case that while the church in Baltimore is scarcely worthy of being considered a cathedral,...it can be regarded as such if one contrasts present conditions with the extreme simplicity of our beginnings.

To put this development into an even wider context, John Gilmary Shea, called the Father of American Church History, once wrote:

> The arrival of priests from France elevated the worship in all the churches. Under the penal laws of England, the Catholic priests in the British dominions had offered the Holy Sacrifice in the simplest manner, and other services were conducted with very little ceremonial. But when clergymen arrived accustomed to see the ritual of the Church carried out with pomp and splendor, and many of them devoted for years to instructing candidates for the priesthood in the ceremonies of religion, with all their beautiful and inspiring suggestions to a devout heart, the old slavish spirit of penal days was discarded: the service of the Church, especially in Baltimore, became grand and imposing: its ceremonial was appreciated and loved.[122]

So, Nagot was an early pioneer in liturgical development in the U.S. Shortly afterwards another French emigré Father Jean-François Moranvillé (1770-

---

120 Ibid.

121 Hanley, I, 466 and 475.

122 John Gilmary Shea, *History of the Catholic Church in the United States.* I (New York: D. H. McBride, 1888), 408.

1824) would build on his work in Baltimore.[123]

Nagot also ministered to individuals in Baltimore. At that time, there was a fairly large population of French-speakers in the city. Some had been there since the French and Indian Wars when the British had forcibly evicted the Acadians from southeastern Canada. Hundreds of them came to Maryland and eventually moved to Baltimore where they established a neighborhood called "French Town" near the harbor.[124] Others, as we have seen, were refugees from the French Revolution and from the slave revolts in Saint-Domingue (Haiti). Nagot ministered to many of these immigrants and also to some Anglophone Catholics in the Baltimore area.[125] He also served the sick during a Yellow Fever epidemic, probably in the mid-1790s.[126]

During his first ten years in the U.S., Nagot corresponded with former students and acquaintances. One, as we have seen, was Candide-Michel Le Saulnier (1758-1830), the pastor of Notre-Dame in Montreal, whom Nagot called his "dear friend."

In addition, Nagot corresponded with former acquaintances like Alexander Dick, the Scottish convert. In January of 1797, Dick wrote to Nagot that he had received the good news from Edgeworth and others that Nagot was in America and that he had not fallen victim to the French Revolution. Then he summarized the story of his conversion and told Nagot that one of the things that Nagot had said to him in Paris turned out to be prophetic, namely "If God converts you, it will be by way of the cross and tribulation."[127] Dick explained that his conversion had indeed been preceded by suffering, namely, a failure in business and a very serious and prolonged problem with his vision. He concluded his letter by asking Nagot to pray for his Protestant wife who was

---

123 Moranvillé arrived in Baltimore in 1794. He soon learned English and joined the choir at St. Peter's Pro-cathedral. A decade later, he became the fifth pastor of St. Patrick's Church in Fells Point where he gained a good reputation for his work in liturgical music. Sulpician Jean-Baptiste David, future bishop of Bardstown (Louisville today), assisted him there. Moranvillé's ministry is detailed in his "Memoir" that was published in five installments. See Campbell, 433-443; 478-481; 524-527; 556-560; and 622-636. See also Faillon, *Histoire*, I, 43.

124 For more information, see Gregory Wood, *The French Presence*, 61-90.

125 [Faillon?], "*Notice sur*," 5.

126 Ibid. Yellow fever must have been an ongoing threat in the areas around the Chesapeake and Delaware Bays throughout the 1790s. In 1793 there was serious epidemic in Philadelphia. At that time, Baltimore accepted refugees from Philadelphia but kept them in quarantine at first. Baltimore also had some cases that year and in 1794. In 1797, Father Floyd died during a yellow fever epidemic in Baltimore. And, in August, 1798, Nagot wrote to Babad that yellow fever had ravaged Philadelphia for a third time and that many had fled the city. He was hosting one of them at the Seminary. Nagot noted that the autumn chill would greatly lessen the danger – yellow fever is mosquito-borne. See F. C. Nagot, Letter to Babad (Baltimore: handwritten document in Nagot correspondence in the Collection of the Associated Sulpicians of the U.S. at the AA, September 8, 1798), 3.

127 Dick, *Reasons*, 43. This was an allusion to Ps. 31, verse 4: "*Versatus sum in misereria mea.*"

prejudiced against Catholicism. We will hear later about the results of Nagot's prayers.

In April of that year Nagot responded and shared the news about Caldwell's return to Calvinism. Nagot also asked Dick to give him more information about his own recent conversion. In his reply of May 1798, [128] Dick shared with Nagot several long passages from an account of his conversion that he had composed. Dick noted in a postscript that Nagot had given him no information about Thayer and he added, "His zeal will no doubt meet with success."[129] In another letter in 1800, Dick noted again that Nagot had failed to give him any news of Thayer. By this time, as we shall see, Nagot would have been less enthusiastic about Thayer's zeal, and he probably decided that silence was the most charitable response to Dick's inquiries.

Nagot also corresponded with Guillaume-Aubin de Villèle, his former penitent/ directee in Paris.[130] As the French Revolution veered to the left in 1792, Villèle, still a seminarian, left France for Germany where he spent the next ten years in exile. He was ordained there around 1793. While in exile, he came to know a group of Catholic emigrés, the most prominent of whom were Princess Adelheid Amelie Gallitzen and Cardinal Louis-Joseph de Montmorency-Laval (1723-1808). Princess Gallitzen became a conduit of communication between Villèle and Nagot.

PRINCESS GALLITZEN

128 For an unexplained reason, Nagot's letter took nine months to reach Dick.

129 Alexander Dick, Letter to F. C. Nagot (Baltimore: AA, May 30, 1798), 1. Dick noted again, in 1800 that Nagot had failed to give him any news of Thayer. See A. Dick, Letter to F.C. Nagot (Baltimore: AA, August 1, 1800), 3.

130 For the following biographical information, see Boullée, "de Villèle."

Princess Gallitzen, a Prussian aristocrat, was the wife of a very prominent Russian diplomat and the mother of Prince Demetrius Gallitzen who entered St. Mary's Seminary in 1792. Not long afterwards, she wrote to Nagot that she had doubts about her son's vocation to the priesthood, but Nagot wrote:

> If this is not a vocation, then there is no standard by which a true vocation can be tested. Never have I led to the altar a young man of whose vocation I was more certain.[131]

While at the Seminary, the young Gallitzen told Nagot about his interest in the Sulpicians. Nagot's wise initial response was, "Refer it to Our Lord."[132] Gallitzen was the second alumnus of the Seminary to be ordained a priest (1795) and he did join the Sulpicians.

Ludovicus Ioseph de Montmorency Laval, Gallus Episcopus Metensis S.R.E. Presbyter Cardinalis creatus a SS.D.N. PIO PP. VI. in Consistorio secreto Palatii Vaticani Feria II. 30. Martii 1789.

CARDINAL MONTMORENCY-LAVAL

Montmorency-Laval, a member of one of the great aristocratic families of France, was first named a bishop at the age of 29. In 1760 he became bishop of Metz and later was also appointed grand almoner of France. In 1789 he was named a cardinal. Three years later, he took refuge in Düsseldorf where Villèle lived in exile. After Villèle's ordination, Montmorency-Laval took him under his wing and appointed him *grand vicaire* of Metz.[133] This was, in effect, an honorary appointment as the French government no long allowed Montmorency-Laval to function as the bishop of his diocese.

There still exist two letters that Nagot wrote to Villèle, one in July of 1792 when Villèle's was in Düsseldorf, and the other in February 1797, when he was in Münster. In the first of these letters, we learn that Nagot was feeling bad about the distressing news that he was receiving about the situation in France. At the same time, he was happy to have just learned from Emery that the Seminary of Saint Sulpice was still in existence. He also spoke of his affection for Villèle,

---

131 Sarah M. Brownson, *Life of Demetrius Augustine Gallitzen, Prince and Priest,* 79-80.

132 Ibid., 93.

133 Villèle never actually acted as a *grand vicaire*. Rather, after he returned to France in 1802, he was appointed to a ministry of preaching in Paris. From there, he became a bishop.

thanked him for his letter, and wrote, "I see that your heart is all for God."[134]

In the second letter, five years later, we learn two things about Nagot. First, he was especially concerned about Emery that year. Nagot had written to him in the spring of 1796 but had received no reply. In fact, Emery was not in Paris at that time. He had travelled to east central France in the fall of 1795 to stay for some time with his family.[135] The second thing that we learn in this letter is that Nagot had largely recovered from the stroke and the bout of malaria but he admitted to Villèle that he was still not able to concentrate for long on important matters. Toward the end of the letter, he invited Villèle to come to the U.S. as a missionary. He wrote:

> What a great need there is in this country for good priests! There are too few to attend to the harvest; and as many come from various places who are aged members of European religious orders, it turns out that our bishop would prefer them far from his flock and they cause him a great deal of annoyance...If you know the language, you and some others, I would invite you, I would urge you to come to our aid.[136]

Not only was Nagot able to keep in touch by letter with some of his European acquaintances and former students, he was also able to visit personally with a few of them. Of course, he saw Mondésir frequently, and Mondésir left us a very memorable description of Nagot from the 1790s.

> [Father Nagot] was a man of rule by taste; by need he loved solitude and prayer. His face was red while he prayed, as in the pictures of the Seraphim. He fatigued himself much at mental prayer which he made on his knees for hours at a time, and with much contention of spirit. As a result he was nervous and needed to be ceaselessly occupied. He did in an animated way whatever he did....Father Nagot was rude to his body. He had no fire in his study. At the end of a meal, he took a glass of cold water. Sober as a good Sulpician, chaste and modest as a 15-year-old girl, discreet, reticent, averse to being questioned; avoiding idle words, always serious and, when he had any

---

134 "*Je vois que votre cœur est tout à Dieu.*" F. C. Nagot, Letter to Villèle, July[?] 23, 1792 (Baltimore: handwritten document in Nagot correspondence in the AA).

135 Gosselin, I, 376.

136 "*Que nous aurions grand besoin dans ce pays-ci de bons prêtres! Il y en a trop peu pour l'étendue de la moisson; et comme plusieurs sont de toutes sortes de pays, qui viennent à un âge avancé des différents ordres religieux de l'Europe, il s'en trouve que notre évêque voudrait bien loin de son troupeau et qui lui causent beaucoup de chagrin.*" See F. C. Nagot, "Letter to Villèle," Feb. 20, 1797 (Baltimore: Nagot correspondence in the Collection of the Associated Sulpicians of the U.S. at the AA).

sorrow, kept it to himself....He was cleanly [sic] in his person and in all that he did. He was straightforward and there was nothing little about him. He could be sociable on occasions.[137]

Also we know that Nagot saw Thayer more than once in the 1790s though there is no evidence that they maintained a significant relationship. In the fall of 1791, Carroll convoked a first diocesan synod and invited Nagot and his friend Delavau to attend. The synod opened on November 7, and Thayer arrived from Boston and began to participate in the meeting on November 10. Since Carroll made Nagot a vicar general after that synod,[138] it is likely that Carroll discussed Thayer with Nagot. So Nagot was probably aware of some of the concerns about Thayer's behavior in the pastoral arena.[139]

Since the Seminary sometimes served as a hostel for priests from out of town, Thayer stayed there during the summer of 1798.[140] During that visit, he was probably seeking a change of assignment from Carroll. The next year Carroll sent him to Virginia and, not long afterwards, to Kentucky where an accusation that he had sexually exploited a woman prompted him to move to Ireland in 1803.[141]

At some point in 1794 or 1795, Nagot had a visit from his notorious former directee Talleyrand, one-time bishop of Autun. Talleyrand, like many other liberal aristocrats, had been forced into exile in 1792 when the revolution in France became so polarized that there was no longer room for mere reformers. First he went to England where he was not able to live in the style to which he was accustomed. In January 1794 he was expelled from there under the new "Aliens Act" aimed at French refugees. At that time, he wrote to another refugee:

It is at age 39 that I begin a new life....America is as good an

---

137 Mondésir, "Souveniers," 1st installment, 23. The translator of this text summarizes it with the words, "Prayed Hard and Kept Busy." Mondésir tended to psychologize about the people he discussed in his *Souveniers.*

138 Nagot was not listed as a vicar general during the synod. However, in an official document, dated Oct. 19, 1793, Nagot's signature is followed by the abbreviation "vic. gen." This shows how quickly Carroll placed his trust in Nagot. See F. C. Nagot, Certification of the Authenticity of Reliques, (Baltimore: handwritten document in Nagot personal papers, Oct 19, 1793). Also, Dilhet wrote much later that Nagot was a vicar general. See Dilhet, 51.

139 See, e.g., Hanley, II, 226. In this letter of December, 1997, Carroll indicated that Thayer communicated with him through Nagot. Also, in a letter of March, 1798, Thayer asks Carroll to give his respects to Nagot. See John Thayer, Letter to John Carroll, March 12, 1798 (Baltimore: handwritten letter in the AA), 2.

140 Tessier, "Historical diary," 3-10.

141 See, e.g., Hanley, II, 340-342. Thayer's character is still a subject of some debate today. On the one hand, some still admire him, e.g., the Coming Home Network International. At the same time, historians have been exposing his serious failings, including sexual misconduct. Carroll had heard rumors about this. See, e.g., John R. Dichtl, *Frontiers of Faith: Bringing Catholicism to the West in the Early Republic* (Lexington, KY: University Press of Kentucky, 2008), 73-77.

asylum as any other. When one has taken courses in political thought, it is a country to see.[142]

So in the spring of 1794 he sailed to Philadelphia, the U.S. capital and the nation's second largest city, where he lived in the company of other prominent French exiles for the next two years.[143] Making money in land speculation, he travelled around the U.S. Perhaps it was on one of those trips that he stopped in Baltimore to see Nagot.

The only record we have of this visit is a short and humorous anecdote about his arrival at the seminary. Garnier, who greeted Talleyrand at the front door, went to Nagot's room to alert the superior. He said to Nagot, "Your former penitent has arrived and he has a long confession to make!" It is unfortunate that we know nothing more about what was discussed during this visit because Talleyrand's future conduct would have a serious impact on the ministry of the Sulpicians in the U.S. We have already seen the damage done by the XYZ Affair in 1797-98. Moreover, in 1803 Talleyrand, representing Napoleon, would sell the Louisiana Territory to the U.S. rather than see it taken over by Britain.[144] This sale would double the size of the already huge Diocese of Baltimore and open the way for DuBourg's appointment as apostolic administrator of Louisiana and the Two Floridas in 1812.[145]

BISHOP DUBOURG

Nagot also seems to have had a hobby during this period. Behind the seminary, on a parcel of extra land that Nagot had purchased early on, he planted a peach orchard "with his own hands."[146] This orchard was located behind the seminary where Paca Street is today.[147] In his diary, Tessier mentioned several times that Nagot was out working in the orchard on a particular day. Sometimes, Tessier reported, Nagot pruned the peach trees and at other times he did some

---

142 Furstenberg, 72.
143 For more information, see Furstenberg, 89-137.
144 Apparently, at about this time, Talleyrand was laicized by the Pope. See Hanley, II, 408.
145 From there he would go on to become bishop of Louisiana and the Two Floridas (1815), bishop of Montauban (1826), and archbishop of Besançon (1833).
146 Mondésir, "Souveniers",h 1st installment, 20.
147 Tessier, *Epoques*, 16.

grafting. This was probably one of Nagot's ways to escape the frustrations that he sometimes faced as the superior: in a peach orchard, progress is more easily attained and its fruit more quickly enjoyed.

XII

Turning Some Corners
(1802-1810)

As we have seen, Nagot's first ten years in the U.S had been a time of hard work and great frustration for him. As the nineteenth century dawned, Nagot seemed to have little hope for the future of the Seminary. Georgetown was not sending seminarians. Yet the opening of St. Mary's College produced so much tension that Nagot and his collaborators were thinking about closing it or moving it far away from Baltimore. Emery was talking about recalling the Sulpicians to France. And Nagot's health had been compromised by serious illnesses.

However, during the next eight years, Nagot's final years as superior, some things finally started to break in his favor. Not only did the Seminary finally begin to grow but Nagot also took successful initiatives to guarantee that it would prosper when he was no longer in charge. And, after one early setback, the College prospered.

The Seminary

During this period, enrollment at the Seminary finally began to increase.[1] There was only one seminarian in 1801, and one in 1802. In the spring of 1803, however, Nagot wrote to his friend Le Saulnier that he had been completely discouraged by the failure of the seminary and was more than willing to return to France, but,

> Providence finally willed that we succeed completely in carrying out our project. It was necessary to battle all sorts of obstacles in order to be where we are today. Here we are in possession of our goal.[2]

That fall, enrollment rose to six, and the following year to eleven.

By 1810 twenty-four seminarians were enrolled. Moreover, many of those enrolled were native-born Americans. While Georgetown had only provided one seminarian during the previous ten years and a second in 1803, four more came from there in 1804.[3] And several students entered after attending either St. Mary's College or the new pre-seminary program that Nagot himself would establish, as we shall see below.

---

1 Ruane, 66.

2 F. C. Nagot, Letter to Le Saulnier, Apr. 20, 1803, trans. L. Bruno (Baltimore: typed document in Nagot correspondence in the collection of the Associated Sulpicians of the U.S. at the AA), 2.

3 Tessier, *Epoques*, 18.

At first, the college students and seminarians lived in the same building. Nagot was not happy with this arrangement. By 1805, he and DuBourg were able to achieve a complete separation of the College from the Seminary, still located in the old inn.[4] This allowed the seminary to have an environment there that Nagot believed was more suited to priestly formation.

The College

After generating much controversy at its inception, St. Mary's College became firmly rooted during this period. At a meeting in December 21, 1801, it was noted, "The thought that we might be recalled, and many other reasons made us decide to keep the Academy [St. Mary's College] in Baltimore." Enrollment grew rapidly and it soon eclipsed Georgetown.[5] However, there was a serious bump along the way.

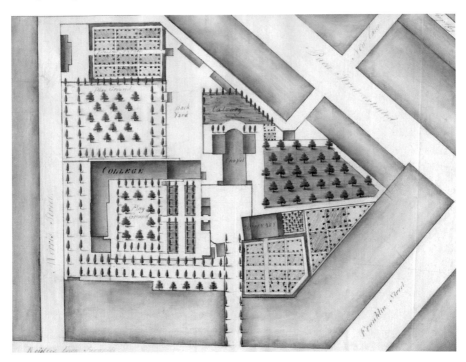

SITE PLAN OF ST. MARY'S SEMINARY & COLLEGE, c. 1820

In the spring of 1802, during a trip to Havana, DuBourg learned that the colonial government there wanted to recall all of the Cuban students from Baltimore. Nevertheless, in 1803, "The Superior [Nagot] proposed to the

---

4 Ibid.

5 Curran, *The Bicentennial History*, I, 56. Curran added that Baltimore was growing quickly and greatly overshadowed Washington at that time.

Fathers that we put into action the purpose we had in founding the Academy, i.e., to form subjects for the ecclesiastical state."[6] At the same time, Nagot and the others began to see that they would have to open the doors of the College to Protestant students if the Cuban students were recalled.[7] When the Cubans finally left on September 20, 1803, the College lost 23 of its 53 students, and DuBourg announced that the College would accept both Catholics and Protestants.[8] Nagot agreed to this decision, realizing that it was necessary for the survival of the College and knowing that Carroll had no objection to the inclusion of Protestants in the student body.[9]

Predictably, the former Jesuits at Georgetown were dismayed, and, a few years later, Georgetown was in danger of closing down.[10] At the same time, this shift in target audience allowed St. Mary's College to resume its rapid growth. In 1805 DuBourg was able to obtain a university charter for the College from the Maryland Legislature. In the following year, there were 106 students and ten instructors.[11]

The rapid growth of St. Mary's College required new facilities. The first was opened in 1804, and, with the seminary enrollment also growing, plans were made to build a proper chapel to serve both institutions. The cornerstone was set on May 17, 1806,[12] and on June 16, 1808, the chapel was blessed by Carroll, newly named an archbishop.[13] On that same day Saint Elizabeth Ann Seton arrived in Baltimore.[14]

---

6 Minutes of the Faculty Meeting, Mar. 26, 1803.

7 Nagot, Letter to Le Saulnier, Apr. 20, 1803, 2.

8 Ruane, 120. DuBourg had done a similar thing at Georgetown in 1798, and it led to an increase in enrollment there.

9 Carroll wrote to Plowden in 1806 that, despite the reservations of some "rigid Sulpicians," he had no objection to having many Protestant students at the College. See Kauffman, 75. Moreover, twenty years earlier, he informed Plowden that he would encourage Catholics to attend non-Catholic colleges, with the hope that some would go on from there to priesthood. See Curran, *The Bicentennial History* 12.

10 Ibid., 58-60.

11 Herbermann, 106. The College was finally suppressed by the Sulpician authorities in France. However, its suppression allowed for the opening of two successor institutions: St. Charles College, a dedicated minor seminary run by the Sulpicians, and Loyola College, today Loyola University of Maryland, run by the Jesuits.

12 Tessier, *Epoques*, 20.

13 In the spring of 1809, Nagot also got approval from the Holy See to name St. Joseph and St. Aloysius Gonzaga as the other patron saints of the Chapel, i.e., in addition to the Blessed Virgin Mary, Saint Sulpice and St. Martin of Tours. See ibid., 25.

14 While the original Seminary and College buildings are long gone, the Chapel of the Presentation of the Blessed Virgin Mary is still a destination for visitors and pilgrims today.

ST. MARY'S CHAPEL IN 1808 BY M. GODEFROY

Pidgeon Hill and Emmitsburg

In 1806 Nagot made what might seem to be a dramatic decision. At the age of 72, he left the day-to-day administration of the campus in Baltimore in the capable hands of his right-hand man Tessier and moved to a farm in the Conawago Valley in southern Pennsylvania, where he created a dedicated minor seminary program. This decision needs some context.

Nagot was pleased to see the College prosper but, after 1803, when the College opened its doors to all applicants, he came to believe that it did not provide the best environment for students preparing to enter the Seminary.[15] To put it another way, the College in Baltimore was no longer enough like the College of Tours that had promoted his own priestly vocation more than a half century earlier. The presence of many Protestant students at the College – they were sometimes in the majority – was clearly one reason for his concern. As he wrote later, "The grouping of Protestant children with Catholic was a major consideration (regarding secular and spiritual formation) that demanded that one proceed with serious thought and especially that one would pray fervently to God for guidance."[16] Moreover, it should be no surprise to learn that he regretted deeply that he and his confreres could do very little to promote the

15 Faillon, *Histoire*, I, 114-115.
16 Nagot, "Memorial," July 31, 1809.

spiritual lives of those young Protestants.[17]

Nagot also expressed another concern that flowed from his Sulpician training. He felt that, to some extent, the College lacked the simplicity that was appropriate for the training of future priests.[18] While admitting that a college "necessarily needs a certain éclat,"[19] he also wrote that it entertained its friends lavishly, was well decorated, and held very grand celebrations on special days. This caused two concerns for Nagot. First, he believed that such an environment worked against the formation of a priest who should be detached and "disinterested" after the model of Christ, "the poorest of men, since he had not a place to lay his head."[20] Second, he felt that some of his confreres, especially DuBourg, enjoyed this environment more than they should have. In this vein, he wrote:

> How can we (especially we to whom God has given such a strong lesson of voluntarily being stripped of all material things and especially of stripping us of everything during the recent Revolution and who should edify in this matter of poverty those whom we educate for the Church) how can we resolve to live and assume a lifestyle of ease which would put us at the same level as the richest families in Baltimore![21]

In this context, it should be noted that some people felt that DuBourg had too much influence over Nagot.[22] Nagot certainly recognized and affirmed DuBourg's ability and energy. Nevertheless, in light of Nagot's later reservations about DuBourg's management of the College, it is fair to say that Nagot felt he should have given DuBourg a bit more supervision.[23]

It is likely that Nagot's concerns about the College were shared to some extent by other Sulpicians, even, to a lesser extent, by DuBourg himself. There are two pieces of evidence for this conclusion. First, just after Nagot moved to southern Pennsylvania in 1806, he sent some boys to Baltimore to be prepared for the priesthood.[24] Despite the fact that they were not yet ready for the Seminary –

---

17 Ibid. 7. See also Ruane, 146-147. Nagot was especially concerned that many of the Protestant boys did not observe Sunday as the Lord's Day. Rather, for them Sunday was just a day off when they could visit their families. At the same time, he was aware of the fact that some Protestant ministers in Baltimore were urging Protestant parents not to send their children to St. Mary's College. See Ruane, 124.

18 Nagot, "Memorial," June 19, 1809.

19 Ibid., 4.

20 Ibid., 9.

21 Ibid., 4.

22 Spalding, *John Carroll*, 45.

23 For example, at one point, Nagot expressed regret that he had not asked the local Sulpicians to draw up some guidelines for the running of the College. See F. C. Nagot, "Memorial," June 19, 1809.

24 They came from better-off families and had better educations. So Nagot thought that they would not fit in well at Pidgeon Hill. See Ruane, 161.

they had not yet finished their study of the humanities – they were not simply placed into the College. Rather, a special program was developed for them: they lived at the Seminary and took classes at the College. "This departure meant the establishment of a veritable preparatory seminary within the grand [major] seminary."[25]

Second, as we shall see, at about this time DuBourg himself was thinking about a way to establish a more permanent, dedicated minor seminary.[26] Perhaps his thoughts were prompted by his recognition that the College was no longer well suited to fulfilling its original purpose.[27]

This is the context for what might seem a surprising decision of Nagot in 1806. However, if this decision is viewed in the light of his life-long concern about the preparation of candidates for the major seminary and in light of his determination to find a good feeder for St. Mary's Seminary in Baltimore, this decision was fully understandable.[28]

FATHER GALLITZEN

The farm that was to be Nagot's residence and a minor seminary for the next two years was located in the Conawago Valley, near a place called Pidgeon Hill (sometimes Pigeon Hill or Pidgeon Hills), about five miles north of Hanover, Pennsylvania. This was a very Catholic area of southern Pennsylvania about 60 miles north of Baltimore. The farm was also only about five miles northeast of the old Conawago Chapel, now the Basilica of the Sacred Heart, where Sulpician Demetrius Gallitzen (1770-1840) had ministered in the late 1790s[29] and where Dilhet had also assisted more recently.

---

25 Ibid., 162.

26 Had DuBourg discussed this with Nagot before his departure to Pennsylvania?

27 Gosselin, II, 382.

28 Seven of the students from Pidgeon Hill entered St. Mary's Seminary, and three were ordained priests. See Cornelius Cuyler, "Pigeon [sic] Hill," *The Borromean*, XIII, no. 6 (Nov., 1947), 6.

29 The Jesuits had evangelized the native peoples living in the Conewago Valley and later served the Catholic population there. Much of the land belonged to the Carroll family (Adams Co. was originally in Maryland), and many German and Irish Catholic immigrants settled there.

A French refugee from Lyons named Joseph Harent (sometimes Heront) had purchased this 273-acre property near Pidgeon Hill on April 4, 1794 as a summer residence which he called "Friendly Hall."[30] Locals called his farm Harentford (or Herontford), and Harent opened a small school for local boys in his large house.[31] He was very close to the Sulpician community in Baltimore and, Nagot, who suffered greatly in the summer from the heat and humidity of Baltimore, had enjoyed visiting him there during vacations.[32]

When Harent returned to France after Napoleon became emperor, he gave Nagot the use of the farm while he was overseas. We will see shortly that, at first, Nagot used the farm as a temporary residence for some Trappist monks from France. When these monks moved out in 1806, the farm was available for another use, and Nagot seized the opportunity to open his minor seminary there. During that summer, he recruited ten local boys, mostly from German families, to enter his new program.[33] Full of hope, on July 6 he wrote as follows to an older

FATHER JOUBERT

seminarian in Baltimore named Jacques (usually James)-Hector-Nicholas Joubert de la Muraille (1777-1743), who had arrived recently from France:

> Nothing could be more pleasing to my old age than the new order that is about to begin in this place. I am delighted; and from day to day I become more pleased when, visiting the boys of this district, I hear them ask to be admitted among the students of the clerical school which we are endeavoring to establish.[34]

---

30 John Timon Reily, *Conewago: A Collection of Catholic Local History* (Martinsburg, WV: Herald Print, 1885), 84. Harent would be ordained in 1812 and would become a Sulpician. His financial acumen helped to save the Seminary during the War of 1812. See Cuyler, 23. He gave his farm to the Society.

31 An unsigned and undated paper in the "Pidgeon Hill" file of the Adams County Historical Society. See also Dilhet,

32 Herbermann, 125. See also Minutes of the Faculty Meeting, Oct., 1801. Father Tessier's diary mentions Harent often. For example, he wrote that Nagot stayed with Harent from September 2-16, 1799, but the weather was terrible. Harent was one of the laymen who gave gifts of food to the seminary, presumably from his farm. See, for example, the entries for Dec. 12, 1797, and Nov. 2, 1796. Tessier's diary is available at the AA.

33 This and most of the following information about Nagot's pre-seminary program comes from Ruane, 159-164.

34 Ibid., 161. Joubert arrived in 1804 and entered St. Mary's Seminary the following year. In 1828 he worked with Mother Mary Lange to found the Oblate Sisters of Providence.

On August 15, he entrusted his enterprise to the protection of the Blessed Virgin Mary.[35] After the school year was under way in the fall of 1806, he gave his students a set of rules appropriate for their age. One rule was, "They must be careful not to abuse any property on the farm, cutting trees, destroying fences, marking benches or trees."[36] They were also forbidden to smoke, chew tobacco, or fight with sticks.

On December 8, he wrote to Carroll:

> I believe that this little institution which God seems to have arranged for my last days has been a rich present of Providence for your diocese. It is also my delight. I am surprised as much as can be at the good health I am enjoying here…Finally, our young seminarians, whom I cherish as my own children, understand perfectly what I presume to tell them in English.[37]

He also wrote to Carroll to reassure him that he was only accepting country boys who would not be eligible for admission into Georgetown.

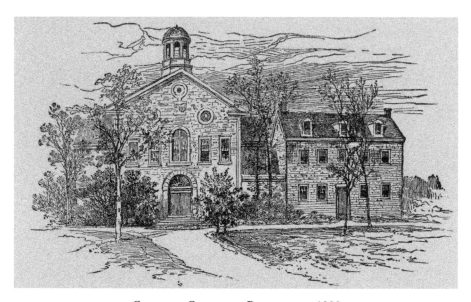

CONEWAGO CHAPEL AND RESIDENCE, C. 1820

---

35 Faillon, *Histoire*, I, 118.

36 Sulpician Archives Bulletin, #86.

37 Ibid., 163. Faillon expressed amazement that Nagot, at his age and with his qualifications, could find joy in running Pidgeon Hill. See Faillon, *Histoire*, I, 122-123.

At first Nagot ran the program with the help of Dilhet and one seminarian from a German family.[38] Shortly afterwards, Dilhet left, and another seminarian was sent up to help him. From then on, he spent much of his time instructing the two seminarians who assisted him. On major feast days, he would march his little community to the Conawago Chapel where they would assist with the liturgy.[39]

Emery wrote to Carroll that he was very pleased with the new enterprise in Pidgeon Hill. Emery said that it was better suited than the College for preparing men for the ecclesiastical state.[40] At the same time, it was clear that Nagot, in his 70s, would not be able to run this program indefinitely. In fact, he hoped that he could turn the school over to his confrere Flaget. However, this plan was thwarted when, in 1808, Flaget was named bishop of the new Diocese of Bardstown, now Louisville, Kentucky.

But another option was opening up. Father Jean Dubois (1764-1842), a talented and zealous young French priest-refugee, asked to enter the Society of Saint Sulpice in 1805. Shortly before, he had been sent by Carroll as a missionary in Western Maryland, and near Emmitsburg, Maryland, he purchased a property of seventeen acres for his own future retirement residence.[41] Later Dubois recalled that in 1807[42] DuBourg had proposed to him the idea of building a minor seminary on his little parcel of land.[43] He agreed to do that but did not want to be the superior of that school. Later that year, Dubois wrote to Carroll and said that one reason that he had offered the land to the Sulpicians was "the uncertain situation of the new little seminary at Conawago."[44]

---

38 Later Dilhet claimed falsely that he founded ("établi par moi-même") the program at Pidgeon Hills. See Dilhet, 73.

39 Mary E. Meline & Edward F. X. McSweeny, *The Story of the Mountain: Mount Saint Mary's College and Seminary*, I (Emmitsburg, MD: Emmitsburg Chronicle, 1911), Ch. II, page, 21.

40 Letter of Emery to Carroll, June 29, 1808, 3. Emery had not been in favor of the admission of Protestants to the College. Like Nagot, he would have preferred more simplicity in a Sulpician enterprise. See Ruane, 121-122.

41 Dubois wrote to Maréchal in 1812 to give him an account of the opening of the Mount. See J. Dubois, Letter to A. Maréchal, Nov. 23, 1812 (Baltimore: handwritten document in the collection of the Associated Sulpicians of the U.S. at the AA), 1. One of Dubois' biographers highlighted the fact that in 1807 Dubois told DuBourg that he did not want to be the one to be responsible for running the minor seminary. See Richard Shaw, *John Dubois: Founding Father* (New York: Catholic Historical Society and Mount St. Mary's College, 1983), 40.

42 Melville thinks that, despite Dubois' personal testimony, DuBourg made this suggestion in 1805, but her reasons for the earlier date are less than compelling. See Melville, 168.

43 There is no record of DuBourg's motivation for doing this. One author has suggested that he was guilty about having diverted the College from its original purpose. See Gosselin, II, 382. It is also possible that he agreed with Nagot that a more focused institution was needed, as it had been in Paris before the French Revolution, and he knew that Pidgeon Hill was not a long-term solution.

44 Jean Dubois, Letter to J. Carroll, Nov. 28, 1807 (Baltimore, Doc. 3 F11 in the collection of the Archdiocese of Baltimore at the AA), 1. This letter mentions the "uncertain situation of the new little seminary at Conawago," and this is compatible with Dubois' recollection that he discussed Pidgeon Hill with DuBourg in 1807.

In April, 1808, after permission had arrived from Emery to accept Dubois into the community but before Nagot interviewed him, the Sulpicians in Baltimore noted:

> M. Dubois offers to give us some land on which he intends to build a church, and also to put up a house which would be a house of retirement and rest for the sick, in a perfectly healthy climate; it is about 18 miles from Fredericktown. We thought of beginning to build such a house according to a plan which would be open to enlarging in case we should decide to establish there a Minor Seminary like that of Pidgeon-Hill.[45]

BISHOP DUBOIS

---

45 Minutes of the Faculty Meeting, Apr. 28, 1807. Meline and McSweeney, Ch. I, seem to indicate that it was Dubois who proposed to build a minor seminary, but Dubois' letter and these minutes show otherwise. Based on Dubois' letter, it may have been DuBourg who convinced the Sulpicians to open the minor seminary. DuBourg may have foreseen that Nagot would not be able to run Pidgeon Hill for long. Nagot recognized this as well.

According to Tessier, in the summer of 1808, Nagot sent Dubois and DuBourg to Emmitsburg to search for additional property for the proposed seminary.[46] Nagot himself also visited Emmitsburg to approve the recommended purchase. On December 6, 1808, it was said, "Today we received him [Dubois] as one of ours, in this meeting, although he is not to live in the Seminary or the College, he will be in charge of building the Minor Seminary at the Mount; we have decided to begin that building in the spring."[47]

In October, 1808, Harent unexpectedly returned from France and it was no longer practical for Nagot to continue his program at Pidgeon Hill for very long. Moreover, Nagot's age was catching up with him. On Feb. 8, 1809, it was noted in the minutes of a meeting,

> It is quite probable that M. Nagot will be unable to return there [Pidgeon Hill] in the near future, because of leg trouble which may last for a long time. That Minor Seminary cannot go on without the presence of one of us. We are forced to stay in Baltimore because of our respective occupations, constant and daily. We noted that we would not see any inconvenience to transferring, as soon as possible, that seminary to the Mount, where there will be a house capable of putting up all those who are at Pigeon Hill. The nearly continual presence of M. Dubois there could make up for M. Nagot's absence.[48]

On March 14, 1809, Nagot was in Baltimore for a meeting, and it was recorded:

> We had already decided to transfer to that location the Minor Seminary of Pigeon [sic] Hill right after Easter. Thus the institution at Mount St. Mary will begin to serve the purpose for which we undertook it, that is to furnish young clerics destined to come to our Baltimore Seminary.[49]

It is usually said that Dubois, a future bishop of New York, was the founder of Mount St. Mary's Seminary. He built the first buildings at the Mount and he was its very capable first Sulpician superior, appointed by Nagot despite Dubois' reluctance.[50] With the assistance of the young Sulpician Simon-Guillaume-Gabriel Bruté de Rémur (1779-1839) who arrived in the U.S. in 1810, he

---

46 Tessier, *Epoques*, 25.

47 Minutes of the Faculty Meeting, Dec. 6, 1808.

48 Ibid., Feb. 8, 1809. In effect, Dubois was assigned to take Nagot's place since there was no one else available at the time. Emmitsburg was only about 25 miles southwest of Pidgeon Hill.

49 Minutes of the Faculty Meeting, Mar. 14, 1809.

50 J. Dubois, Letter to A. Maréchal, Nov. 23, 1812.

overcame many hardships in service to the Mount.[51] However, in light of the passages above, to call him the founder, without qualification, would be to ignore the fact that he was acting under the authority of Nagot and the Sulpician community in Baltimore.[52] Moreover, it was Nagot who went to the Mount in April of 1809 to bring his students and program to the Mount. So again, Nagot played a critical role in founding an important Catholic institution. As Faillon wrote, "M. Nagot himself laid its [the Mount's] foundations" at Pidgeon Hill.[53]

Emery's Last Years

During the years 1802 to 1810, Napoleon was first consul and then emperor of France. These were also the years when the Society of Saint Sulpice in France was revived and then suppressed again. This era ended when the Society laid to rest the man who had led it through most of the hardships of the Revolution and the Napoleonic era. World events again had an impact on Nagot, but two concerns related to Emery were finally resolved: Nagot would remain in the U.S., and the college would be accepted as a Sulpician program.

The Concordat with Napoleon, signed in September of 1802, was good news for the Society of Saint Sulpice in France. Emery was able to reopen the seminary in Paris and repurchase many properties there that had been confiscated during the Revolution. Moreover, at the request of various bishops, he began to reopen Sulpician seminaries around the country.[54]

Nevertheless, the Concordat was not entirely good news for the Sulpicians in the U.S. because it led to the recall of some of them to France. At about

---

51 Bruté was named first bishop of Vincennes, now Indianapolis, in 1834. Bruté loved to draw and he left us two skethes of Nagot at the time of his death, as we shall see later.

52 This was acknowledged in a way by Meline and McSweeney, 3-4, when they wrote, "He [Dubois], with them [the Sulpicians], was destined to found Mount St. Mary's College." Melville says that, from one perspective, DuBourg was the Mount's founder. See Melville, 169. She presents the minor seminary as wholly his idea. However, her minimizing Nagot's role is based largely on an argument from silence.

53 [Faillon?], *Cahiers*, 4.

54 At Emery's request, the Sulpicians in Baltimore sent him some funds to assist in this task.

that time, Charles-François d'Aviau du Bois de Sanzay (1736-1826), the new archbishop of Bordeaux, needed a superior for his seminary that was about to reopen. He wrote to Emery in 1802, who replied that he was thinking about sending Nagot who was about to be recalled from overseas.[55]

A contemporary of Nagot, Aviau was from a noble family but did not attend the Sulpician Seminary in Paris. Rather he had his seminary formation under the Sulpicians in Angers.[56] In 1790 Aviau was named archbishop of Vienne but he was forced into exile not long afterwards. Back in France in 1802, he was named archbishop of Bordeaux and so he had had the very difficult task of rebuilding the local Church there after the devastation caused by the Revolution. Recognizing his lack of clergy, he quickly turned his attention to reopening the archdiocesan seminary. He wanted a Sulpician as superior, but, in the end, Emery had no one to send him at the time.[57] Nevertheless, Nagot and Aviau maintained a good relationship and corresponded during the next decade, sometimes discussing the pastoral problems of Bordeaux and sometimes discussing theology.[58]

ARCHBISHOP AVIAU

In September of 1802 Emery convoked the first general assembly of the Society since 1790. So sure were he and the assistants that Nagot would be one of those returning to France that, on October 15, the assembly elected him as the second regular consultor of the Society.[59] Since, at that time, he had been in the U.S. for more than eleven years and since he was not a participant in that assembly, Nagot's election was clear testimony to the esteem that the leadership of the Society still had for him. The letter no longer exists in which Emery

---

55 L. Bertrand, *Histoire des séminaires de Bordeaux et de Bazas*, (Bordeaux: Feret, 1894), II, 12. Faillon wrote that Aviau asked for Nagot. [Faillon?], "*Notice sur*," 4.

56 For information on the early life of Archbishop Aviau, see Jean-Paul-François Lyonnet, *Histoire de Mgr d'Aviau Du Bois de Sanzay* (Lyon: J. B. Pelagaud, 1847), vol. I.

57 See ibid., II, 635. Aviau did eventually succeed in getting the Sulpicians to run his seminary, but that was not until after Emery's death. See ibid., 635-636.

58 See the letters from Aviau in the Collection of the Associated Sulpicians of the U.S. at the AA, in Nagot correspondence.

59 Minutes of the General Assembly, III, 123ff.

recalled Nagot and informed him of his election.[60] However, the news probably hit Nagot as a mixed blessing. On May 23, 1803, during the spring sailing season, Garnier and Levadoux left for France. In his diary, Tessier added, "The superior was to leave with these gentlemen, but since he was unable to complete preparations in time, he found it necessary to remain."[61] Maréchal sailed for France shortly afterwards from Philadelphia,[62] but Nagot was still not ready to leave,[63] and so he missed the entire spring-summer sailing season in 1803.

In February, 1804 Emery wrote to Nagot inviting him to come back to Paris that spring if his health allowed ("*si sa santé le lui permet*").[64] Tessier commented:

> Father Nagot is restrained from doing so by his poor health and by the attendant difficulty of finding a ship which might provide the comforts necessary for the voyage. In addition, the almost certain hope that we have of establishing a seminary here is a powerful motive for keeping him in Baltimore.[65]

Although Nagot's reply no longer exists, Emery must have been satisfied to allow him to remain in the U.S., at least for the time being. As we have already seen, it was just at this time, that seminary enrollment began to increase rapidly. Then on December of 1804, Emery sought guidance from Pope Pius VII who was in Paris for Napoleon's coronation as emperor. The Holy Father asked Emery to give the Seminary in Baltimore more time and so he finally dropped his plan to recall all of the Sulpicians from the U.S. That settled Nagot's future.

PIUS VII AT THE CORONATION OF NAPOLEON I

60 There is a note, signed by Emery and dated Jan. 16, 1803, that says that Nagot was invited (*invité*) to return with Levadoux, Garnier, and Marechal. See Minutes of the General Council, III, Jan. 16, 1803.

61 Tessier, *Epoques*, 14.

62 See Nagot, Letter to Le Saulnier, Apr. 20, 1803, 1. For one thing, Nagot did not want to cross the Atlantic in another small brig. Maréchal would return to the U.S. in 1812 and in 1817 he would be consecrated by Cheverus as the third archbishop of Baltimore.

63 See Nagot, Letter to Le Saulnier, Apr. 20, 1803, 1. Aviau wrote that Nagot was indisposed ("*incommode*") at the time Marechal sailed. See Bertrand, *Histoire des séminaires*, II, 15.

64 Minutes of the General Council, "1804."

65 Tessier, *Epoques*, 16.

At the beginning of this period, Emery was still expressing displeasure about St. Mary's College. However, in 1806, Carroll finally persuaded him to drop his opposition. The College was growing very quickly, and Carroll had informed Emery that he had no objection to the presence of Protestants there.[66] So Emery finally relented and accepted the College as a Sulpician program under Nagot's authority.[67]

Meanwhile, back in France, all was not going well. Though Napoleon had signed the Concordat, he had no intention of allowing the papacy to have significant influence in his domains. It was as if he wanted all the privileges granted by the Concordat of Bologna, and more, but he did not accept the kinds of concessions that Francis I had once made to the pope. In 1808 Napoleon invaded Rome, and in 1809 he annexed the Papal States and took Pius VII prisoner.

During this period, Emery weighed in more than once on behalf of the papacy, and this angered some of Napoleon's ministers. Emery had some standing because of his leadership of the archdiocese of Paris and because of his public

service. Moreover, Emery had been responsible for helping Napoleon's uncle, Joseph Fesch (1763-1839), to return to priestly ministry after his military service in the Napoleonic Wars, and in 1803 Fesch was named a cardinal. Nevertheless, on May 12, 1810, Emery warned Nagot that it was possible that the Society of Saint Sulpice might be suppressed again and that many confreres might be sent to America.[68] Emery was right: the Society was suppressed for a second time on June 13, 1810. "Emery, perhaps from the shock of this final trial, died on April 28, 1811, at the age of 79."[69]

CARDINAL FESCH

---

66 Ruane, 123-124. Emery had thought for some time that it was not the mission of the Sulpicians to run a college for Catholics and Protestants, that such an institution was not suitable for preparing men for the priesthood.

67 For a time, Emery had viewed it as DuBourg's own personal ministry. See ibid., 113.

68 Faillon, *Histoire*, I, 175-176.

69 Molac, 118.

BISHOP HAY

During this period, Nagot began to publish again. The first of his works during this period was published in Paris in 1808. It was a French translation of *The Scriptural Doctrine of Miracles Displayed*, a two-volume work first published in 1775 by the Scottish Bishop George Hay (1729-1811).[70] Hay, a convert and a disciple of Challoner, was a vicar apostolic in Scotland during the penal period, but he survived to see the dawn of relief legislation. He was also the sponsor of a Scottish institute in Paris that was destroyed during the French Revolution.

FATHER BUTLER

Then, three years later, Nagot published his French translation of *The Moveable Feasts, Fasts and Other Annual Observances of the Catholic Church* by the English Catholic historian Father Alban Butler (1710-1773),[71] a work that, after Butler's death, was revised by Challoner and published at his request. Butler had been a professor at the English College in Douai, his alma mater in the north of France. After the suppression of the Jesuits there, he served as the president of the English College at St-Omer. Since his *The Moveable Feasts* was intended to be a supplement to his famous *Lives of the Saints*, Nagot's translation was republished in 1811 as

---

70 George Hay, *La doctrine de l'écriture sur les miracles, où l'on examine et on développe avec impartialité leur nature*, trans. F. Nagot. 3 Vols. (Paris: Sourds-Muet, 1808).

71 Alban Butler, *Fêtes mobiles, jeûnes et autres observances annuelles de l'Église catholique,* trans. F. Nagot. Versailles: J.-A. Lebel, 1811.

the final volume of a new French edition of this much larger work.[72]

These two translations say a lot about Nagot's personal and intellectual interests during his years in the United States: they were still focused on priestly formation and evangelization. Nagot was already working on Hay's book late in 1803. We know this because, in January of 1804, Nagot's Scottish convert Alexander Dick mentioned in a letter that he was pleased to hear from Nagot that he had such a high opinion of Hay that he was translating one of Hay's works.[73] And we know that Nagot began translating Butler's work even before that since this project had been mentioned by Mondésir who left the U.S. for France in 1801.[74]

One recent summary of *The Scriptural Doctrine of Miracles Displayed* helps to show how it coincided with Nagot's passions.

> Miracles were to be regarded as absolute proofs of divine communication. In fact, Hay argues that the Protestant Reformation could be rejected on the grounds that it wrought no miracles to prove the legitimacy of its innovations...Hay made no attempt to persuade skeptics or deists that miracles are possible or historically demonstrable. His arguments were directed at Protestant moderates who already believed in the possibility as well as the fact of miracles. He argued that if any Christian miracles are worthy of belief then Roman Catholic miracles must be among them, for why should the establishment of the original gospels be the only function of miracles?[75]

Nagot's translation of *The Moveable Feasts* was also in line with his main interests. Butler, like Hay and Challoner, was another 17th-century Catholic intellectual whose life was deeply influenced by British penal legislation. Because that legislation prohibited Catholic education on all levels in England, Butler's whole academic career took place in the Low Countries and in the north of France. His writings on the saints and on devotion to them were designed to present an essential aspect of traditional Catholic piety to his English-speaking

---

72 Butler, Alban; Godescard, Jean-François; Marie, Joseph-François; and Nagot, Charles. *Vies des pères, des martyrs, et des autres principaux saints: tirées des actes originaux et des monumens les plus authentiques, avec des notes historiques et critiques.* New edition in 14 volumes. Versailles: J.-A. Lebel, 1811.

73 Dick, 202. As we already saw, Dick had been admitted to the Catholic Church by Hay. In a letter to Nagot in April 1804, Dick gave Nagot some information about Hay's conversion. See A. Dick, Letter to F. C. Nagot (Baltimore: Nagot correspondence in the AA, April 30, 1804), 1-2.

74 Mondésir, "Souveniers," 3rd installment, 23.

75 Jeffrey M. Suderman, *Orthodoxy and Enlightenment: George Campbell in the Eighteenth Century* (Montreal: McGill University, 2001), 211-212.

readers.[76] Challoner probably promoted the posthumous publication of *The Moveable Feasts* because it complemented his own long quest to revive the liturgical celebration of important English saints.[77] As an historian once wrote, Challoner and his friend Butler "did more than any of their contemporaries in preserving the faith amongst men of their own generation, and in promoting conversions to the Church."[78]

Nagot also translated other works into French, but none of them was published. Not surprisingly, most were instructional and/or apologetic works by Challoner and Hay.[79] He also translated similar works by Jesuits of the Catholic Reformation, namely the Englishman Robert Persons (also Robert Parsons, 1546-1610), a pioneer in the Jesuit English missions;[80] the brilliant Spaniard Juan Eusebio Nieremberg (1595-1658);[81] and, if Bertrand is right, the prominent Hungarian theologian Martin Szentiványi (1663-1708).[82] These translations must have occupied much of Nagot's spare time in the U.S. and may have been related to his teaching of seminarians.

In Nagot's mind, what pastoral need did these translations address? Virtually all of these books had been written for Catholics in Great Britain in the 17th and 18th centuries. Why were French versions needed in the early 19th century? The reasons is that, after the devastation caused by the French Revolution, parts

---

76 Sometimes Butler was criticized for his excessive belief in the miraculous, but this would not have been a problem for Nagot.

77 The renewal of the cult of the saints also played an important part in the revival of the Church in France after the Napoleonic period.

78 William R. B. Brownlow, *A Short History of the Catholic Church in England* (London: Catholic Truth Society, 1895), 463. It is interesting to know that, when Thayer wrote of his own conversion, he cited the example of saints and holy people like Madame Louis as confirmation of the truth of Catholicism. See J. Thayer, A Letter to His Brother, in *The Conversion of the Reverend John Thayer, etc.* (Hartford: U.S. Catholic Press, 1832), 35.

79 These were: Challoner's *Considerations Upon Christian Truths and Christian Duties*, *The Catholic Christian Instructed in the Sacraments, Sacrifices, Ceremonies and Observances of the Church by Way of Question and Answer*, *The Grounds of the Catholick Doctrine*; and Hay's *The Sincere Christian Instructed In The Faith Of Christ From The Written Word*, and *The Pious Christian Instructed in the Nature and Practice of the Principal Exercises of Piety Used in the Catholic Church.*

80 This was Person's *Christian Directory, Guiding Men to Eternall Salvation.*

81 The title of Nieremberg's original Spanish work was, in English translation, *A Treatise of the Difference Betwixt the Temporal and Eternal*. It was published several times in English from 1793 on.

82 Bertrand wrote that Nagot translated Szentiványi's 1708 Latin work entitled, *Quinquaginta rationes et motiva cur in tanta varietate religionum et confessionum fidei in christianitate moderno tempore vigentium, sola religio Romano-catholica sit eligenda et omnibus aliis preferenda*. However, in Nagot's time, there was a work in English with a very similar title that was attributed to Duke Anton-Ulrich von Brunswick (Braunschweig)-Lüneburg (1663-1714), a prominent convert to Catholicism in 1709-1710 who wrote a justification of his conversion shortly afterward. See the English version entitled, *Fifty Reasons or Motives, Why the Roman Catholick Apostolick Religion ought to be Preferr'd to all the Sects this Day in Christendom* (Antwerp, 1715). This work was reprinted in 1801 in Dublin and in 1802 in England and it was republished several more times in the 19th century. Because of its popularity in English-speaking countries, this is more likely to have been the work that Nagot translated under the title, *Cinquante raisons ou Motifs de préférer la religion Catholique, Apostolique et Romaine, à toutes les autres sectes de ce jour dans la Christianisme.*

of France were missionary territory. So Nagot probably saw his translations as contributions to the revival of the Church in his home country. During that period, for example, most of the religious orders and apostolic communities, including the Sulpicians, the Jesuits and the Daughters of Charity, were being revived, and new orders and communities, like the Oblates of Mary Immaculate and the Little Sisters of the Poor, would be founded. Lay confraternities also thrived.

Nevertheless, the diocesan priesthood was in disarray. "Not only had levels of ordination plummeted to an all-time low, but many clergy had been driven from the ministry, and those who remained were for the most part aged, infirm and inactive."[83] As the seminary system was being rebuilt, vocations were coming less from the upper and middle classes and more from the rural poor. Though dedicated, these new priests were less well educated than their 18th-century predecessors, and it took some time before Catholic intellectual life would flower again in France. So Nagot's translations of solid catechetical and apologetic works that were written for another context were probably intended to aid this new generation of diocesan priests in re-evangelizing their parishioners.

Other Experiences

Nagot continued to receive French refugees at the seminary. One group of visitors were Trappists. Their Superior Dom Augustin [Louis-Henri] de Lestrange (1754-1827) had been a seminarian at the *Robertins* from 1772-1778, and Nagot, superior of the *Petit Séminaire* at the time, was very likely his confessor/ director.[84] In June, 1792, Lestrange wrote to Nagot, his "true friend," about the suffering being caused by the French Revolution.[85] The abbey of La Trappe in lower Normandy had been nationalized and the community suppressed.[86] So the monks fled to French speaking Switzerland and, under the leadership of Lestrange, established a new monastery at La Val Sainte.

---

83 See N. Atkin and Frank Tallett, *Priests, Prelates and People: A History of European Catholicism since 1750* (Oxford: Oxford University, 2003), 114.

84 Arsène Christol, O.C.S.O., "Dom Augustin de Lestrange (1754-1827)," 25. At http://www.arccis.org/ downloads/lestrange.pdf (accessed 11/18/15). Lestrange wrote to Nagot in 1811, "How happy I would be had I been able to see you once more, as I had hoped, and to profit from the last counsels of the one who on so many occasions was a support in my youth." See Gabriel Bertoniere, *Through Faith and Fire, the Monks of Spencer 1825-1958* (New York: Yorkville Press, 2005), 474.

85 A. de Lestrange, Letter to F. C. Nagot, June 1, 1792. (Baltimore: AA, Nagot correspondence).

86 Recall that the revolutionaries saw no social utility in the contemplative life.

ABBAYE DE LA TRAPPE AVANT LA RÉVOLUTION. (p. 5)

THE ABBEY OF TRAPPE BEFORE THE FRENCH REVOLUTION

DOM AUGUSTIN DE LESTRANGE

He wrote to Nagot again in 1795, after he became superior general of the growing community, and told him that Emery had recommended to him that he authorize a new foundation in Canada or in the U.S.[87] Lestrange began by sending two groups to Montreal, but both stopped on the way at safe places in Europe and established houses there.[88] He also considered the U.S. a possible place of refuge.

During Napoleon's initial conquests in 1798, the Trappists were driven out of Switzerland and wandered all over Europe for the next few years as they tried to find a safe permanent home. In 1802, after they were ejected from Russia because they were French,

---

87 A. de Lestrange, Letter to F. C. Nagot, Sept. 11, 1795 (Baltimore: AA, Nagot correspondence).

88 See Anonymous, *"Projet d'un établissement de Trappistes en Amérique,"* a document from Les archives de l'abbaye de la Trappe, ALT, cote 55 - pièce 39, At http://www.abbaye-tamie.com/histoire/documents-trappistes/trappistes-amerique-1794-1815/projet-amerique.doc/view, 1 & 7 (the pages are not numbered).

Lestrange sent a group to the U.S. under the leadership of Dom Urbain Guillet (1764-1817). That September, Nagot warmly welcomed Guillet and his 24 companions who had just arrived from Holland after a difficult voyage. A description of their arrival at the Seminary, composed by one of the visitors, shows that it was not just in his correspondence that Nagot was warm and caring:

> It was very hot, and when we arrived the gentlemen [i.e., the Sulpicians] were in the yard near the house, seated on benches and talking together. As soon as they saw us, they came to greet us. Mr. Nagot, a venerable octogenarian [sic], was the first, with a very confident step, to extend his arms to us in the most warmhearted manner and to speak the friendliest words. He embraced us one-by-one. As he went on speaking, you could see tears of joy running down his cheeks. The demeanor of the other gentlemen was in complete harmony with what Mr. Nagot said and did.[89]

Guillet and his companions remained in Baltimore for some time. Then Nagot invited them to live at Herant's farm in south-central Pennsylvania. As we have already seen, when Napoleon came to power and France gained some stability, the homesick Harent went back to France but, before he left, he gave Nagot permission to use the farm as he wished while he was away.

So the Trappists lived at Pidgeon Hill for three years. In July, 1805 they moved to Kentucky where, with help from Father Stephen Badin, the first alumnus of the Seminary, they found what seemed to be a more suitable location. After a series of setbacks and disappointments, Guillet and some other Trappists ended up in New York where they joined Lestrange in exile. He had refused to take an oath of loyalty to Napoleon in 1811, and the Emperor had put a price on his head.[90] Nagot may have helped him raise money for his journey to the U.S.[91] When Napoleon fell, both Lestrange and Guillet returned to France. In 1847 the Trappists would return to Kentucky where they would be welcomed by the Sulpician Bishop Benedict Flaget who had been present in Baltimore for Guillet's visit forty-five years earlier.

---

89 *Il faisait très chaud et quand nous arrivâmes, ces Messieurs étaient dans la cour près de la maison, assis sur des bancs à converser ensemble. Aussitôt qu'ils nous aperçurent, ils vinrent à notre rencontre. M. Nagot vénérable octogénaire, allait le premier, d'un pas très assuré, nous tendant les bras de la [11] manière la plus affectueuse et nous adressant les paroles les plus aimables. Il voulut nous embrasser tous les uns après les autres. Il parlait toujours et en même temps, on voyait couler sur ses joues des larmes de joie. La contenance des autres Messieurs était aussi parfaitement d'accord avec ce que disait et faisait M. Nagot.* See ibid., 10.

90 Ibid., 29-30.

91 See A. de Lestrange, Letter to Nagot, 1811 (Baltimore: Nagot correspondence in the AA). This appears to be a kind of "case statement" that Nagot could use with potential donors.

Nagot also continued to correspond with Alexander Dick. One long and interesting letter from Dick concerning his wife and brother has survived.[92] On January 28, 1804, he wrote, "Let me now hasten to give you the consolation you wish for and to tell you that your prayers for my dear wife have not been in vain – she has been a Catholic since last St. Andrew's day."

Dick went on to explain to Nagot that two incidents had led to her decision to join the Church. The first was the apparently miraculous recovery of her daughter from a serious illness just after she had turned to God in prayer, "adding that if her prayers were heard she would regard it as a proof that the Catholic religion was true." The second incident, shortly afterwards, was the sudden conversion of his 26-year-old brother during a serious personal crisis:

> I return to Mrs. Dick. My brother's extraordinary (to you, I may say, miraculous) conversion completed also the victory of grace in her soul. She was received into the Church, and in all appearance her mother also will soon follow her example.

Dick added that, after his brother's conversion, Dick shared with him a letter from Nagot that described the visit of the Trappists to Baltimore. This had a profound effect on the brother because he was already in the process of discerning a vocation to monastic life.

Dick also visited Nagot in Baltimore during this period. In 1816 Dick composed a short addendum to the account of his conversion. In it, he wrote about the visit as follows:

> I had the happiness of seeing my venerable friend in that country [the U.S.] in the year 1807. Old age and infirmities had then begun to make inroads on his bodily frame, but his mind, his heart, his affections, were the same as ever.[93]

Nagot was also visited by Bishop-elect Jean-Louis Lefebvre de Cheverus (1768-1836), an alumnus of Saint Sulpice in Paris and another French émigré, who arrived in Boston from England in 1796. In 1808, he was appointed the first bishop of Boston.

92Alexander Dick, "Copy of a letter, dated Edinburg, 28th January, 1804, to the late venerable Mr. Nagot," *The Metropolitan* (Baltimore: T. Blenkinsopp, 1830), 200-204.

93 Dick, *Reasons for Embracing*, "Note A – Page 57," n.p.

Cardinal Cheverus

The bulls having at length arrived [in 1810], he went to the Seminary in Baltimore, to prepare himself for his consecration by private exercises of devotion. These he performed under the direction of M. Nagot, the Superior of the establishment, an old man venerable for his angelic virtue, his amiable simplicity, and his deep humility.[94]

As bishop, Cheverus would sometimes ask to have his regards extended to Nagot, and his first biographer wrote in 1839:

> The great affection that the Bishop of Boston entertained for the Jesuits was extended also to the priests of St. Sulpicius [sic]; he was intimate with all the directors of the Seminary at Baltimore, but more particularly with the Superior, M. Nagot, whom he venerated as a saint, and loved as a father.[95]

Cheverus visited the seminary at other times, and we know from Tessier that he presided at some ordinations and installations later on.[96] He was recalled to France in 1823 where he served first as bishop of Montauban and then as cardinal-archbishop of Bordeaux, succeeding Aviau.

---

94 J. Huen-DuBourg (André-Jean-Marie Hamon), *The Life of Cardinal Cheverus,* trans. E. Stewart (Boston: James Munroe, 1839), 94. See also Christian de Jouvencel, ed., *Cardinal de Cheverus (1768-1836): Lettres & Documents* (Viroflay, France: chez Christian de Jouvencel: 2005), 132-133.

95 Ibid., 125. When he preached at the episcopal consecration of Flaget in 1810, he quoted words that the famous Bishop François de Salignac de la Mothe-Fénelon (1651-1715) had said on his deathbed: "I know nothing more venerable and more apostolical [sic] than the order of Saint Sulpicius." See Ibid. 85.

96 See, for example, Tessier, *Epoques,* 36.

SAINT ELIZABETH ANN SETON

The best known person whom Nagot came to know during this period was Saint Elizabeth Ann Seton (1774-1821). With the encouragement of DuBourg, she moved from New York to Baltimore along with her family. She arrived on May 17, 1808, the day that St. Mary's Chapel was dedicated. Until June of 1809, she lived in a newly built house just behind the Seminary. She conducted her first Catholic school in that house, and she worshipped in the crypt of the Chapel along with other Catholics in the neighborhood. There she took her first vows.

MOTHER SETON'S HOUSE TODAY

Although there are no records of her interactions with Nagot while she was living in Baltimore, they undoubtedly got to know each other, and she developed a great affection for him. Carroll had appointed him as the priest-superior of her new community, and in a letter of May, 9, 1809, she wrote of him as follows:

The Superior of our Seminary here…is graced with all the venerable qualities of seventy five which is his age, a mind still strong and alive to the interest of our little family as if we were all his own, and one of the most elegant men in his manners you ever met with.[97]

A week later, in another letter, she called him "our dear dear dear cherished beloved Father," In letters to Carroll that year, she would refer to him as "holy Mr. Nagot."[98]

Failing Health and Resignation

Nagot must have recovered fairly well from his life-threatening illnesses during the 1790s, but he was never as strong as before. In 1803, for example, when Nagot was 69, Carroll wrote to Emery to discourage him from recalling Nagot to France, In that letter, Carroll wrote:

> I believe that he [Nagot] could never survive the fatigue of a new journey. His spirit has not the same force and activity that you used to know.[99]

Also, there is much evidence that the hot and humid summers in Baltimore were particularly hard on Nagot during this period. In the fall of 1805, for example, Carroll wrote to Garnier in France, "Even Mr. Nagot looks much better, since the heats [sic] ceased." [100] And in February of 1808, when Nagot was at Pidgeon Hill, Carroll wrote to Maréchal, also back in France,

> The venerable Mr. Nagot [was] no longer able to bear the heat of Baltimore….He enjoys there [Pidgeon Hills] health and tranquility which sweeten his last days."[101]

However, as Nagot approached 75, his health became less stable. On August 17, 1808, Tessier wrote, "Father Nagot, being very ill and thinking that he was near the end, received Holy Viaticum"[102] And in May of 1809, Saint Elizabeth Ann Seton described Nagot's condition as follows:

---

97 Elizabeth A. Seton, *Elizabeth Bayley Seton: Collected Writings*, eds. J. Bechtle and J. Metz (New York: New City Press, 2002), II, 69.

98 Ibid., 71, 91 & 107.

99Hanley, II, 404. Carroll added, "His example and his authority which his virtue preserve for him, render him ever necessary here."

100 Ibid., 492.

101 Hanley, III, 43.

102 Tessier, *Epoques*, 25.

Father [Nagot] is running his heavenly race with a swiftness which I believe will soon put him beyond our view, except some additional bodily strength is given him - he faints almost intirely [sic] sometimes three or four times a day every thing he eats however simple creates indigestion and pain which is often so acute that I expect him to give up his spirit while they are on him. but such a mind! all activity purity and joy rejoicing in Suffering and triumphing in the cross always hoping that the sufferings of the Pastor will be accepted for his flock — [103]

On June 12, Nagot himself wrote, "stomach pain, pain more severe than ever, and the constant nausea have been a serious warning for me to think daily that death is near at hand and to prepare for it in a special way."[104]

Yet, on July 31, he wrote that he was finally feeling somewhat better, and so he continued to lead the community as he was able. On August 14, 1809, Carroll wrote to Garnier, "The Venerable Mr. Nagot…suffers as usual in the summer from his nervous affections: notwithstanding which, he arrived this morning at the Seminary from Conewago and walked over this afternoon to pay me his visit."[105] Yet, four days later, Carroll changed his tone in a letter to his sister Elizabeth, writing, "The Venerable Mr. Nagot, Superior of the Seminary and of all the Sulpicians here, is to all appearances closing his most holy life. I go to see & be edified by him every day."[106]

During this prolonged period of recurring illness, Nagot wrote to Emery again and asked that he be allowed to resign as superior. Emery told him that he would allow it if Carroll agreed. Nagot hoped that this time Carroll would let him resign.[107] So Nagot wrote to Carroll in July, 1809, giving nine reasons for his request![108] He argued, among other things, that his illness forced him to focus exclusively on his health and so he was distressed to still have duties as a superior which he was no longer able to fulfill. Near the end of his plea, we find these words: "All of this, My Lord, authorizes me, I think, to want to be able to withdraw for a while to prepare for the end of my pilgrimage."

In Carroll's response, written on the back of Nagot's request, Carroll said that

103 Elizabeth A. Seton, *Elizabeth Bayley Seton: Collected Writings*, II, 71.

104 Nagot, "Memorial," 1.

105 Hanley, III, 90-91. Carroll added, "Hi[s-*torn*] seems to be already in heaven; for I think, that he does not for one minute lose sight of his God."

106 Ibid. 92. Recall that Nagot had once described his stroke as a "nervous disorder."

107 F.C. Nagot, Letter to J. Carroll, July 1, 1809 (Baltimore, Nagot correspondence in AA), 1.

108 F. C. Nagot, Letter to J. Carroll, n.d. (Baltimore: AA, Nagot correspondence) and J. Carroll, Letter to F. C. Nagot, September 23, 1809, (Baltimore: Nagot correspondence in the AA).

Nagot's request caused him "pain and disquietude" because he considered Nagot "endowed with singular gifts of God to preserve religious discipline in the Seminary, and to teach others the practice and rules of Christian self denial." But out of concern for Nagot's health, his discomfort with continuing as superior and his "earnest supplication," Carroll consented to his resignation at the end of the school year.

Later that year, Saint Elizabeth Ann Seton wrote that Nagot was well enough to sing the High Mass on the 50th anniversary of his ordination to the priesthood.[109] He was 75. However, contrary to her wishes, his health did not permit him to accompany her to Emmitsburg to guide her community there.

In light of Carroll's response to Nagot's request during the summer of 1809, one would have expected Nagot to step down as superior after his 50th Anniversary, i.e., at the end of the 1809-1810 school year. However, that did not happen, probably because Carroll asked him to stay on for a while longer. Yet, early in the next school year, Nagot became even more determined to resign. He was 75 years old and he had been a superior for close to forty years. Here is Tessier's description of Nagot's formal resignation itself on November 8:[110]

> The Archbishop had graciously accepted our invitation, together with the Coadjutor-Archbishop and the three new Bishops [Cheverus, Flaget, and Egan]: they all dined at the Seminary. All the Gentlemen and the students of the seminary gathered in the large hall of the College, with the Gentlemen of the College plus a few members of the city clergy and a few pious laymen. M. Nagot reminded the Archbishop of the oft-repeated insistence he had made, following the authorization of the Superior-general, to accept his resignation, and he renewed that request in the most urgent manner. The Archbishop said that he believed he should finally give in to M. Nagot's prayers: [sic] since the final decision had been placed in his hands, he accepted the resignation, after telling M. Nagot of the feelings he had towards him...The Archbishop expressed the wish that M. Nagot continue to preside at the community exercises, and to begin and end the prayer customarily said at those exercises, at least for a time.

Then Carroll, following the wishes of Emery, announced the appointment of Tessier as the new superior. Nagot presided at community prayer only until

---

109 Tessier, *Epoques*, 26.
110 Minutes of the Faculty Meeting, Nov. 9, 1810.

the twentieth of the month when he insisted on giving up every mark of the superiorship.[111]

It seems fair to say that, at the time of his resignation, and despite his recent illnesses, he must have felt some satisfaction in knowing that the Seminary in Baltimore had finally gained traction and that the minor seminary, now at the Mount, gave it good prospects for the future.[112]

111 Ruane, 93-94.
112 A similar conclusion was offered by Faillon. See [Faillon?], *Cahiers*, 4.

XIII

FINAL YEARS
(1811-1816)

The final five years of Nagot's life also marked the end of a period of western history. In Europe those years saw the end of the Napoleonic Era. In 1812 Napoleon conducted his Great Retreat from Moscow, and in 1814 he was exiled to Elba. In the spring of 1815, he returned to power but was finally and decisively defeated at the Battle of Waterloo on June 18, 1815.

The exile of Napoleon to Elba in 1814 enabled the Society in Paris to get a new lease on life. There was a general assembly in Paris that September, and Antoine du Pouget Duclaux was elected as the new superior general. Duclaux began immediately to work toward the legal reinstatement of the Society, and in 1816 he received *lettres patents* approving the Society's new statutes.

FATHER DUCLAUX

In the United States these years were dominated by The War of 1812 with Britain that secured once and for all the independence of the U.S. from its colonial master. The war came about this way. While Napoleon was at war in Europe, the U.S. struggled to benefit from trade. However, aggressive British actions on land and sea led Congress to declare war on June 18, 1812. Though for some time the war was inconclusive, Napoleon's abdication enabled the British to mount a major invasion of the Chesapeake region in 1814. Tessier wrote:

Toward the end of August, of this same year [1814], the city of Baltimore was in turmoil [sic] and fright, especially after the English had burned the public buildings in Washington. We expected every day to see the enemy arrive. However, they did not do so until the 10th of September; during the night of the 14th, they made a terrific attack from the sea, but were repulsed with losses; and their general [Robert Ross], by a stroke of good fortune, having been killed in the land attack, they withdrew on the 15th and did not return any more.[1]

THE DEATH OF GENERAL ROSS NEAR BALTIMORE (COURTESY OF MdHS)

These years of dramatic political events were the final years of Nagot's life. In 1811 he was back in the ministry of spiritual direction, and "all were greatly edified to see the former Superior of the house take his place in the ranks and show himself obedient to the point of asking with the simplicity of a young seminarian for the least permission."[2]

We have four items of information about Nagot in 1811. First, for most of the year, his health seemed reasonably stable. He regularly attended meetings with his confreres during that year, and, along with them, he signed a letter to Emery requesting additional personnel for Baltimore. However, Tessier recorded that on March 9, Nagot fell down the steps and bled profusely. His confreres thought he was going to die, but he recovered, though for a while afterwards he suffered from the effects of a concussion and/or a mild stroke.[3]

Second, in Paris at this point Emery was losing hope that the Society would be revived in France, and this highlighted for him the importance of the work of the Society in North America. So during the spring of 1811, Emery wrote

---

1 Tessier, *Epoques*, 30. Major General Ross (1766-1814) was a veteran of the Napoleonic Wars and the leader of the assault on Washington. He was killed by a sniper at the Battle of Northpoint.

2 Ruane, 94. Ruane took these words from Nagot's obituary. See [Antoine Garnier?], "Necrologie," 3.

3 Tessier, *Epoques*, 27. It seems at least possible, given Nagot's medical history, that a minor stroke was the cause of the fall. Tessier indicated that afterwards Nagot had difficulty concentrating.

to Nagot about his idea of uniting the Sulpicians of North American under one Sulpician leader who would become a vice superior general of the Society. Surprisingly, in March and April, he told Nagot that he was contemplating asking him to take this position until his death (*"pendant que vous vivrez"*).[4] Emery was not yet ready to act on this idea when he himself died on April 28, 1811.

Third, Nagot continued to share his thoughts with Emery. In a letter of May 17, 1811, Nagot wrote that, despite his recent fall, God again gave him a few more days (*"encore quelques jours"*) so that he could prepare properly for death.[5] He went on to draw a contrast between the situation in the U.S., where Divine Providence had blessed the contribution of St. Sulpice to a young Church, and the situation in France, where the Society was no longer able to pursue its mission of service to the Kingdom of God.

This letter was written about three weeks after Emery's death, but the news of his death did not arrive in Baltimore until the summer. The seminary celebrated a solemn memorial Mass for Father Emery on Oct. 5, 1811, at the beginning of the school year. Tessier reported, "The Archbishop and all the clergy of the city were present."[6] Presumably, Nagot was present as well.

Finally, despite his fall in March, he continued to assist as he was able with pastoral ministry in the Archdiocese. The Pastor of Saint Patrick's Church Father Moranvillé, a French émigré who had known Nagot since the 1790s, gave the following description of a Corpus Christi celebration at his parish on June 16, 1811: "Under a rich silken canopy, the sacred host, in a brilliant ostensorium, was born by the venerable Nagot, whose devout demeanor, and venerable head whitened by the snow of many years, inspired respect even in those who did not know how profound was his learning, and transcendent his virtue."[7] Nevertheless, Carroll commented to a friend, "When I read your account of the Ven. Mr. Nagots [sic] exertion on Corpus Christi day & the following Sunday, I attributed his bodily power to the ardor of his charity."[8]

During 1812 Nagot's long and difficult final decline began. He was no longer recorded as attending meetings with his confreres. One source says that when he was no longer able to work, he spent a great deal of time before the Blessed Sacrament, and everyone was edified by his resignation and by his strong desire

---

4 Gosselin, II, 314.

5 See F. C. Nagot, Letter to Emery, May 11, 1811 (Baltimore: handwritten document in Nagot correspondence in the collection of the Associated Sulpicians of the U.S. at the AA), 1.

6 See Tessier, *Epoques*, 28.

7 Campbell, 559.

8 Hanley, III, 152.

to return to Jesus Christ.[9]

Then, he began to experience mental deterioration, manifested by periods of confusion and incoherent speech. During that summer, Tessier wrote, "Father Nagot has nearly lost his mind; difficulty in connecting his thoughts."[10] Surprisingly, he added, "His health otherwise has been good." In February 1814, Tessier wrote in his diary, "M. Nagot is so weak, especially in the head, that he usually has to stay in bed; he has not said Mass since January 9."[11]

On November 22, 1815, Tessier wrote, "M. Nagot is getting weaker and weaker." So he was probably not able to join the other members of seminary community on November 24, when they were present for Carroll's reception of Viaticum and the Last Anointing. On December 3, 1815, Carroll died at the age of 80, and Tessier wrote that three days later he was solemnly laid to rest in the crypt of the Chapel in a burial chamber that had been prepared originally for Nagot's body.

On January 2, 1816, Nagot, 81, had another fall. He was discovered on the floor in his room and "he was delirious the whole day."[12] During the next few days he continued to have spells of delirium. On January 5 he was "lost all day."[13] On January 6 he received the Last Anointing in the presence of the whole community, and on the 14th he received Viaticum. However, he rallied once again.

Then on March 12 the severe weakness returned, and he received Viaticum again. For weeks he lingered, losing consciousness at one point. His last brief rally took place on Palm Sunday, April 7, and he was able to receive the Sacrament of Penance and Holy Communion that day. By the evening he was failing again, and on the next day he was no longer able to communicate. "On April 9, he gave up his soul to God at about 8 o'clock in the morning, without agony, without any convulsion or motion, like a person who peacefully goes to sleep."[14]

---

9 "…*édifiant tout le monde par sa constante résignation, et par le vif désir qu'il témoignait d'aller se revenir à Jesus Christ.*" See [Faillon?], "*Notice sur,*" 6.

10 Tessier, "Historical diary," June 20, 1813.

11 Tessier, "Historical diary," Feb. 3, 1814.

12 Tessier, *Epoques*, 32.

13 Tessier, "Historical diary," Jan. 5, 1815.

14 Tessier, *Epoques*, 32. There was only a short notice of his death and funeral that was published in Baltimore newspapers. Tessier also described Nagot's last days in the letter to the superior general. See J. Tessier, Letter to A. Duclaux, April 17, 1816 (Baltimore: RG 24, Box 7, in the Collection of the Associated Sulpicians of the U.S. at the AA).

FATHER NAGOT AT HIS GRAVE (BY BRUTÉ)

Archbishop Neale presided at Nagot's funeral on April 10. At first Nagot's remains were buried in the small cemetery behind the Chapel. In 1824, Carroll's body was removed from the crypt of St. Mary's Chapel and placed in the crypt of the new Cathedral of the Assumption. Later, Nagot's remains were moved from the cemetery to the place where Carroll's body had been. Nagot's remains are still there today under the simple marble slab inscribed in Latin as he had requested in 1810.[15] In English translation, the inscription reads:

---

15 Faillon, *Histoire*, II, 209.

FATHER NAGOT IN DEATH (BY BRUTÉ)

†

IHS

Here lies

Francis Charles Nagot

First Superior of the Seminary of Baltimore:

Born in Tours in France

20 April 1734;

Died 9 April 1816,

Awaiting the coming of the glory of the great God.[16]

Pity me, Pity me,

Especially you, my friends.[17]

R.I.P.[18]

---

16 Titus 2:13. Characteristically, Nagot wanted his epitaph to contain words from sacred scripture.

17 Job 19:21. This is a verse from a reading in the Office of the Dead. It has been taken as an appeal from those in purgatory, who, like the suffering Job, are sustained by their belief that their Redeemer lives. In his "Instructions for His Epitaph," he affirmed his belief in Purgatory. See F. C. Nagot, "Untitled Instructions."

18 The Latin text reads: *"Hic jacet Franciscus Carolus Nagot, primus Seminarii Baltim. Superior: Natus Turonibus in Gallia 20 Aprilis 1734: Obiit 9 Aprilis 1816. Expectans beatam spem et advenium gloria magni Dei. Miseremini mei, Miseremini mei, Saltem vos, Amici mei. R.I.P."*

SULPICIAN PROVINCIAL FATHER JOHN KEMPER SHOWS
FATHER NAGOT'S TOMB TO CARDINAL J. FRANCIS STAFFORD

CONCLUSION

Father Nagot's official obituary, published in France, stated that, when he died, he was considered to be a saint (*"il passa…avec la réputation d'un saint"*), and it contains the following tribute to him:

> M. Nagot had living faith, profound humility, a tender devotion to the Blessed Sacrament; his principle qualities being a habitual union with God, a great gift of prayer, a singular attraction to Holy Scripture which he read and meditated upon constantly, a burning zeal for the salvation of souls and especially for the sanctification of priests. He had much insight for the direction of consciences, and a great ability to proclaim the word of God….It seemed that Jesus Christ spoke through his mouth.[1]

FATHER GARNIER AS SUPERIOR GENERAL

---

1 *M. Nagot avoit une foi vive, une humilité profonde, une tendre dévotion au saint Sacrement, une union habituelle avec Dieu, un grand don de prière, un attrait singulier pour l'Écriture sainte qu'il lisoit et méditoit sans cesse, un zéle ardent pour la salut des âmes et surtout pour la sanctification du clergé étoient ses qualités principales. Il avoit beaucoup de lumière pour la direction des consciences, et un grand talent pour annoncer la parole de Dieu…Il semble que Jésus Christ parloit par sa bouche.* [Garnier?], 288.

The words of Superior General Antoine Garnier, written to the Sulpicians in Baltimore twelve years later, provide a fitting close to this biographical study of Father François-Charles Nagot:

> Remember that there is no vocation more sublime, more beneficial in its effects and more necessary to the Church, than the vocation of a Director of a Seminary....We cannot fulfill such a great destiny unless we follow in the footsteps of our Fathers, of Mr. Olier, DeBretonvilliers [sic], Tronson and the first priests of the Society. You did not know those venerable men, but you had, as your founder and first Superior, an excellent priest full of their spirit, and I do not hesitate to offer as a model that saintly Mr. Nagot, whose virtues and precious death in the eyes of God left their mark on your house. Imitate his simplicity, poverty, regular life, obedience, his spirit of prayer, and his zeal for the salvation of souls.[2]

---

2 A. Garnier, Letter to the Sulpicians at St. Mary's Seminary in Baltimore, Jan. 15, 1828, trans. anonymous (Baltimore: typed document in the file entitled "PSS Seminary, U.S. Province, Seminary Visitation Reports," in the collection of Associated Sulpicians of the U.S. at the AA).

BIBLIOGRAPHY

BOOKS & PARTS OF BOOKS

Atkin N. and Frank Tallett. *Priests, Prelates and People: A History of European Catholicism since 1750.* Oxford: Oxford University, 2003.

Alger, John Goldworth. *Napoleon's British Visitors and Captives, 1801-1815.* New York: J. Pott, 1904. GB

A Convert [Alexander Dick]. *Reasons for Embracing the Catholic Faith.* Edinburgh: R. Marshall, 1848; and London: Dolman, Jones, and Burns, n.d.

Anonymous, "Historical Sketch," in *Memorial Volume of the Centenary of St. Mary's Seminary of St. Sulpice, 1-36.* Baltimore: John Murphy, 1891.

Anonymous, *Recueil par ordre de dates, contenant tous les Comptes rendus par MM. les Commissaires du Parlement, au sujet des Collèges, etc.* Paris: P.G. Simon, 1766. GB

Bachelier, Alcime. *Le Jansénisme à Nantes.* Anger: Imprimeurie de l'Anjou, 1934; and Paris: Nizet et Bastard, 1934.

Barnard, H. C. *Education and the French Revolution.* London: Cambridge U. Press, 1969; republished 2009.

Baston, Guillaume-André-René. *Mémoires de l'abbé Baston, chanoine de Rouen.* 3 vols. Paris: Picard et Fils, 1897. GB

Bayley, James Roosevelt. *Memoirs of the Right Reverent Simon Wm. Bruté, D.D., First Bishop of Vincennes.* New York: J. S. Shea, 1860.

Bayley, James Roosevelt. *The Life of Simon William Gabriel Bruté.* London: Burns & Oates, n.d.

Berchet, Jean-Claude. *Chateaubriand.* Paris: Gallimard, 2012.

Bertoniere, Gabriel. *Through Faith and Fire, the Monks of Spencer 1825-1958.* New York: Yorkville Press, 2005.

Bertrand, Louis, *Bibliothèque sulpicienne; ou, Histoire littéraire de la Compagnie de Saint-Sulpice,* 3 vols. Paris: A. Picard, 1900.

_____. *Histoire des séminaires de Bordeaux et de Bazas,* 2 vols. Bordeaux: Feret, 1894. GB

Boisard, Pierre. *La compagnie de Saint Sulpice; Trois siècles d'histoire.* Paris: Society of Saint Sulpice, n.d.

Bossard, Clément. *Histoire du serment à Paris.* Paris: Chez tous les marchands des nouveautés, 1791. GB

Boullée, M. S. *"de Villèle,"* in *Biographies contemporaines, I, 229-233.* Paris: Auguste Vaton, 1863.

Brownlow, William R. B. *A Short History of the Catholic Church in England.* London: Catholic Truth Society, 1895.

Brownson, Sarah M. *Life of Demetrius Augustine Gallitzen, Prince and Priest.*

New York: Pustet, 1873.

Brugger, Robert J. *Maryland: a Middle Temperament: 1634-1980.* Baltimore: Johns Hopkins, 1988.

Butler, Alban. *Fêtes mobiles, jeûnes et autres observances annuelles de l'Église catholique.* trans. F. C. Nagot. Versailles: J.-A. Lebel, 1811.

Butler, Alban; Godescard, Jean-François; Marie, Joseph-François; and Nagot, Charles. *Vies des pères, des martyrs, et des autres principaux saints: tirées des actes originaux et des monumens les plus authentiques, avec des notes historiques et critiques.* New edition in 14 volumes. Versailles: J.-A. Lebel, 1811.

Carron, Guy-Toussaint-Julien. *Pensées ecclésiastiques pour tous les jours de l'année,* 5th ed., 12 vols. Paris: Rusand, 1823. GB

Chalmel, Jean-Louis, *Histoire de Touraine jusqu'à l'année 1790,* 4 vols. Paris: H. Fournier, 1828. GB

Chateaubriand, François-Rene de, *Chateaubriand's Travels in America*, trans. R. Switzer. Lexington, KY: University of Kentucky Press, 1969.

_____. *"Mémoires d'Outre-Tombe,"* I, in *Oeuvres Completes de Chateaubriand,* XIII, 1-315. Paris: Garnier Frères, 1904 BnF

_____. *"Voyage en Amérique"* in *Oeuvres Completes de M. le Vicomte de Chateaubriand,* vol. 12, 11-310. Paris: Pourrat Frères, 1834. GB

Condorcet, Antoine-Nicolas de. *Outlines of an Historical View of the Progress of the Human Mind.* trans. Anonymous. Chicago: G. Langer, 2009.

Cordina, Gabriel, "The *Modus Parisiensis*," in Vincent J. Duminuco, ed., *The Jesuit Ratio Studiorum: 400th Anniversary Perspectives,* 28-49. New York: Fordham University Press, 2000.

Courbon, Noël. *Instructions familières sur l'oraison mentale.* ed. François-Charles Nagot. Paris: Lottin, 1777.

Courcy, Henry de. *The Catholic Church in the United States: Pages of Its History.* 2nd, ed. N.Y.: Edward Dunnigan & Son, 1857

Curran, Robert Emmett., "'Splendid Poverty: Jesuit Slaveholding in Maryland, 1805-1838," in *Catholics in the Old South,* eds. R. Miller and J. Wakelyn, 125-146. Macon, GA: Mercer University, 1983.

_____. "Rome, the American Church and Slavery," in *Building the Church in America,* eds. J. Linck and R. Kupke, 30-49. Washington: The Catholic University, 1999.

_____. *Papist Devils: Catholics in British America, 1574-1783.* Washington, DC: Catholic University of America, 2014.

_____. *The Bicentennial History of Georgetown University*, 3 vols. Washington, DC: Georgetown U., 1993.

Currier, C. W. *Carmel in America 1790-1890.* Darien, IL: Carmelite Press, 1989.

Dabert, Joseph-Nicholas. *Vie de Mr Vernet, Prêtre de Saint-Sulpice.* Lyons:

Perisse, 1848. BnF

Daley, John M. *Georgetown University: Origin and the Early Years.* Washington, DC: Georgetown U., 1957.

Delarc, Odon. *L'église de Paris pendant la révolution Française, 1789-1801,* 3 vols. Paris: Desclée, de Brouwer, 1895. GB

Deslandres, Dominique, Dickenson, John A., and Hubert, Ollivier. *The Sulpicians of Montreal: A History of Power and Discretion, 1657-2007.* Trans. Steven Watt. Montreal: Wilson and LeFleur, 2013.

Devailly, Guy. *Le diocèse de Bourges.* Paris: Letouzey & Ané, 1973.

Dichtl, John R. *Frontiers of Faith: Bringing Catholicism to the West in the Early Republic.* Lexington, KY: University Press of Kentucky, 2008.

Dilhet, Jean. *État de l'église catholique ou Diocèse des États-Unis de l'Amérique septentrionale.* trans. Patrick Browne. Washington, DC: Salve Regina Press, 1922.

Diesbach, Ghislain de. *Chateaubriand.* Paris: Perrin, 1998.

Durand, Yves, "*La faculté de théologie de Nantes,*" in Gérard Emptoz, ed. *Histoire de l'université de Nantes, 1460 1993,* 48-59. Rennes: Presses Universitaires de Rennes, 2002.

_____. *Le Diocèse de Nantes.* Paris: Beauchesne, 1985.

Edgeworth de Firmont, Henry Essex. *Letters from the Abbé Edgeworth to His Friends, Written between the Years of 1777 and 1807.* London: Longman, Hurst, etc., 1818.

Edgeworth, C. S, ed. *Memoirs of the Abbé Edgeworth, Containing His Narrative of the Last Hours of Louis XVI.* London, Rowland Hunter, 1815. GB

Faillon, Étienne-Michel. *Vie de M. Olier, foundateur de séminaire de S. Sulpice,* 1st ed., 2 vols., Le Mans: Richelet; Paris: Poussielgue-Rusand, 1841.

Feller, François Xavier de. *Biographie universelle,* 65 vols. Besançon: Outhenin-Chalandre, 1838. GB

Follenay, Joseph Paguelle de. *Monsieur Teysseyrre: sa vie, son oeuvre, ses lettres.* Paris: Poussielgue Frère, 1882. BnF

Franklin, Benjamin, *Writings of Benjamin Franklin,* Vol. IX, ed. A. Smythe. New York: Haskell House, 1970. GB

Furstenberg, François. *When the United States Spoke French: Five Refugees Who Shaped a Nation.* New York: Penguin Books, 2014.

Gill, Natasha. *Educational Philosophy in the French Enlightenment: From Nature to Second Nature.* Surrey: Ashgate, 2010.

Glaire, Jean-Baptiste. *Dictionnaire universel des sciences ecclésiastiques,* 2 vols. Paris: Poussielgue, 1868. GB

Gomez-Le Chevanton, Corinne. *Carrier et la Révolution français.* Nantes: Geste, 2004.

Gosselin, Jean-Edme-Auguste. *Vie de M. Emery, neuvième supérieur du Séminaire et de la Compagnie de Saint-Sulpice,* 2 vols. Paris: A. Jouby, 1861.

Grandmaison, Charles de. *Procès-verbal du pillage par les Huguenots des reliques et joyaux de Saint Martin de Tours.* Tours: Mame, 1863. GB

Grégoire, P., *Ètat de diocèse de Nantes en 1790* Nantes: Forest & Grimaud, 1882. GB

Guilday, Peter. *The Life and Times of John Carroll.* New York: The Encyclopedia Press, 1922.

Halls, W. D. *Education, Culture and Politics in Modern France.* Oxford: Pergamon, 1976.

Hanley, Thomas O'Brien, ed. *The Carroll Papers,* 3 vols. Notre Dame: University of Notre Dame, 1976.

Hay, George. *Doctrine sur les miracles, traduit de l'Anglais de Georges Hay, vicaire Apostolique en Ecosse, 3* vols. Trans. F. C. Nagot. Paris: Ange Clo, 1808.

Hayes, Kevin J. *Jefferson in His Own Time: A Biographical Chronicle of His Life.* Iowa City: University of Iowa Press, 2012.

Hemphill, Basil. *The Early Vicars Apostolic of England, 1685-1750.* London: Burns & Oates, 1954.

Henrion, Mathieu-Richard-Auguste. *Histoire des ordres religieux.* Brussels: La Société nationale pour la propagation des bon livres, 1838. GB.

Herbermann, Charles G. *The Sulpicians in the United States.* New York: The Encyclopedia Press, 1916.

Hélyot, Pierre. *Dictionnaire des ordres religieux,* ed. M.L. Badiche. Vol. 3 of L'Abbé Migne, *Encyclopédie théologique,* 22 vols. Paris: Ateliers Catholique de Petit-Montrouge, 1850. BnF

Huen-DuBourg, J. (André-Jean-Marie Hamon). *The Life of Cardinal Cheverus.* Trans. E. Stewart. Boston: James Munroe, 1839. GB

Jauffret, Gaspard-André-Joseph. *Mémoires pour servir à l'histoire de la religion à la fin du XVIIIe siècle.* Paris: Le Clère, 1803. GB

Jedin, Hubert, ed. *History of the Church,* Vol. VI. New York: Crossroad, 1981.

Jouvencel. Christian de, ed. *Cardinal de Cheverus (1768-1836): Lettres & Documents.* Viroflay, France: Chez Christian de Jouvencel, 2005.

Julia, Dominique. *"L'éducation des ecclésiastiques aux XVIIe et XVIIIe siècles"* in *Problèmes de l'histoire de l'éducation.* Rome: L'École française de Rome et l'Università di Roma,1985.

Kauffman, Christopher J. *Tradition and Transformation in Catholic Culture: The Priests of Saint Sulpice in the United States from 1791 to the Present.* New York: Macmillan, 1988.

Kenneally, Finbar. *United States Documents in the Propaganda Fide Archives: A Calendar,* 1st Series, I. Washington: Academy of American Franciscan History, 1966.

Kley, Dale K. Van. *The Religious Origins of the French Revolution: from Calvin to the Civil Constitution, 1560-1791.* New Haven: Yale University, 1966.

Lecot, Victor-Lucien-Sulpice, *Abbé Nollet de Pimprez.* Noyon: Couttu-Harlay,

1865. BnF

LeNotre, Georges. *Les noyades de Nantes*. Paris: Perrin, 1912.

Liptak, Dolores. *Immigrants and Their Church*. New York: Macmillan, 1989.

Lyonnet, Jean-Paul-François. *Histoire de Mgr d'Aviau Du Bois de Sanzay*, 2 vols. Lyon: J. B. Pelagaud, 1847. GB

McManners, John. *Church and Society in Eighteenth-Century France*, 2 Vols. Oxford: Oxford University, 2003.

_____. *French Ecclesiastical Society under the Ancien Régime*. Manchester, UK: Manchester U. Press, 1970.

McLauglin, J. Fairfax. *College Days at Georgetown and Other Papers*. Philadelphia: J. B. Lippincott, 1899. GB

Marcade, August. *Talleyrand: prêtre et évêque*. Paris: Rouveyre et G. Blond, 1883, at http://www.le-prince-de-talleyrand.fr/marcade.pdf (accessed 10/17/2015)

Martin, A. Lynn. *The Jesuit Mind: The Mentality of an Elite in Early Modern France*. Ithaca, New York: Cornell, 1988.

Marty, Martin E., "The American Revolution and Religion, 1765-1815," in *The Cambridge History of Christianity*, Vol. VII, eds. S. Brown and T. Tackett, 497-516. Cambridge: Cambridge University Press, 2006.

Meline, Mary E. & McSweeny, Edward F. X. *The Story of the Mountain: Mount Saint Mary's College and Seminary*. 2 vols. Emmitsburg, MD: Emmitsburg Chronicle, 1911.

Melville, Annabelle. *Louis William DuBourg*. Chicago: Loyola University Press, 1986.

_____. *Elizabeth Ann Seton: 1774-1821*, ed. Betty Ann McNeil. Hanover, PA: Sheridan Press, 2009.

Méric, Élie. *Histoire de M. Emery et de l'Église de France pendant la Révolution*, 5th ed., Vol. I. Paris: Poussielgue, 1895. GB

_____. *Le clergé dans l'ancien régime*. Paris: Lecoffre, 1890. GB

Molac, Philippe. *Histoire d'un dynamisme apostolique: La Compagnie des prêtres de Saint-Sulpice*. Paris: Cerf, 2008.

Mondésir, Jean-Édouard Piarron de. *Souvenirs d'Édouard de Mondésir...[1789-1811]*, ed. Gilbert Chinard. Baltimore: Johns Hopkins, 1942.

Montagu, Violette M. *The Abbé Edgeworth and His Friends*. London: Herbert Jenkins, 1913.

Nagot, François-Charles. *Relation de la conversion de quelques Protestans*. Paris, Prevôt et Crapart, 1789. GB

_____. *Relation de la conversion de Mr. Thayer, ministre Protestant*. N. American ed. (Quebec: Louis Germain, 1795).

_____. *Recueil de conversions remarquables, nouvellement opérées dan quelques protestans*. 2nd ed. Paris: Crapart, 1791; 3rd and expanded ed., Paris, 1796; new and expanded ed., Lyon, Rusand, 1822; new and expanded ed., Lyon: Rusand, 1829; new and expanded ed. Clermont-Ferand: Hubler, 1855. GB.

_____. *Vie de M. Olier, curé de Saint-Sulpice.* Versailles, J. A. Lebel, 1818.

Ott, Alexandre. *Sur l'instruction primaire: l'ancien régime, la révolution, l'époque actuelle.* Nancy: Imprimerie Nanciénne, 1880.

Pasquier, Michael. *Fathers on the Frontier: French Missionaries and the Roman Catholic Priesthood in the United States, 1789-1870.* New York: Oxford, 2010.

Péronne, Joseph-Maxence, *Vie de Monseigneur de Simony: évêque de Soissons et Laon.* 2nd ed. Paris: Louis Vivès, 1861. BnF

Reher, Margaret M. *Catholic Intellectual Life in America.* New York: Macmillan, 1989.

Reily, John Timon. *Conewago: A Collection of Catholic Local History.* Martinsburg, WV: Herald Print, 1885. GB.

Rousseau, Pierre. *Saint-Sulpice et les mission catholiques.* Montreal: Edouard Garand, 1930.

Rouvroy, Louis de, Duc de Saint-Simon. *Mémoires de Saint-Simon, nouvelle édition.* Paris: Librarie Hachette et Cie, 1897. BnF

Ruane, Joseph William. *The Beginnings of the Society of St. Sulpice in the United States (1791-1829).* Baltimore: The Voice of the Students and Alumni of St. Mary's Seminary, 1935.

Seton, Elizabeth A. *Elizabeth Bayley Seton: Collected Writings.* eds. J. Bechtle and J. Metz. New York: New City Press, 2002.

Sàcquin, Michèle. *Entre Bossuet et Maurras: L'Antiprotestantisme en France de 1814 à 1870.* Paris: École des Cartes, 1998.

Schroth, Raymond A. *The American Jesuits: A History.* New York: New York University, 2007.

Shaw, Richard. *John Dubois: Founding Father.* New York: Catholic Historical Society and Mount St. Mary's College, 1983.

Shea, John Gilmary. *History of the Catholic Church in the United States.* 4 vols. New York: D. H. McBride, 1888.

_____. *Memorial of the First Centenary of Georgetown College, D.C., Comprising a History of Georgetown University.* Washington: P. F. Collier, 1891.

Spalding, Thomas W. *John Carroll Recovered.* Baltimore: Cathedral Foundation, 2000.

_____. *The Premier See: A History of the Archdiocese of Baltimore, 1789-1994.* Baltimore: Johns Hopkins University, 1989.

Suderman, Jeffrey M. *Orthodoxy and Enlightenment: George Campbell in the Eighteenth Century.* Montreal: McGill University, 2001.

Tackett, Timothy, "The French Revolution and Religion to 1794," in *The Cambridge History of Christianity,* Vol. VI, eds. S. Brown and T. Tackett,

536-555. Cambridge, UK: Cambridge University Press, 2006.

Thayer, John. *An Account of the Conversion of the Reverend Mr. John Thayer, Lately a Protestant Minister, at Boston in North-America, who Embraced the Roman Catholic Religion at Rome, on the 25th of May, 1783* (London: Goddard, 1788).

_____. *Narratio conversionis Johannes Thayer, etc.* Translated into Latin from the French translation of F. C. Nagot. Münster: Monasterii Westphalorum, 1794.

_____. *The Conversion of the Reverend John Thayer, etc.* Hartford: U.S. Catholic Press, 1832.

Thompson, Edward H. *The Life of Jean-Jacques Olier, Founder of the Seminary of St. Sulpice.* New and enlarged ed. New York: Burns & Oates, 1886.

Walsby, Malcolm. *The Printed Book in Brittany 1484-1600.* Leiden: Brill, 2011.

Wood, Gordon S. *Empire of Liberty: A History of the Early Republic, 1789-1815.* Oxford: Oxford University, 2009. (Kindle edition)

Wood, Gregory A. *The French Presence in Maryland: 1524-1800.* Baltimore: Gateway Press, 1978.

Woodgate, M. V. *The Abbé Edgeworth (1745-1807).* Dublin: Browne & Nolan, 1945.

Anonymous. "Archbishop DuBourg." *Jesuit, or, Catholic Sentinel*, No. XIX (May 10, 1834), 147-148, at http://newspapers.bc.edu/cgi-bin/bostonsh?a=d&d=jcsthree18340510-01.2.4 (accessed Oct. 10, 2015).

Anonymous. "*Eglise Catholique du Maryland.*" *Annales de la religion et du sentiment, Seconde Anné* (1792), no. 6, pp. 129-147. GB

Anonymous. "Etymologie et Histoire de Nantes," at http://www.infobretagne.com/nantes.htm (accessed 8/12/15).

Anonymous, "John Edwards Caldwell: First Agent General of the American Bible Society," *Bible Society Record*, Vol. 51 (Feb. 1906), 28-29. GB

Anonymous, "Life expectancy in France," at https://www.ined.fr/en/everything_about_population/graphs-maps/interpreted-graphs/life-expectancy-france/ (accessed 11/2/2015).

Anonymous. Obituary for François-Charles Nagot in *Catholicon: or, the Christian Philosopher*, III (July-Dec., 1816). London: Keating, Brown and Keating, 1816, 80.

Anonymous, "*Projet d'un établissement de Trappistes en Amérique*," a document from Les archives de l'abbaye de la Trappe, ALT, cote 55 - pièce 39, at http://www.abbaye-tamie.com/histoire/documents-trappistes/trappistes-amerique-1794-1815/projet-amerique.doc/view (accessed 10/2/15).

Anonymous. Review of "Letter of Abbé Edgeworth to his Friends, etc." *The Annual Biography and Obituary for the Year*, Vol. 4. London: Longman, Rees, etc., 1820, 448-449.

Anonymous. Review of Alexander Dick, *Reasons for Embracing the Catholic Faith* (Edinburgh: Marshal, 1848; London: Dolman, Jones, and Burns, n.d.). "Shorter Notices," *The Rambler*, Vol. I, no. 7 (Feb. 12, 1848), 124. GB

Anonymous, "Sodality" at http://www.newadvent.org/cathen/14120a.htm (accessed 9/24/15).

Anonymous, "*Un peu d'histoire*," at at http://seminaire-nantes.cef.fr/un-peu-dhistoire/ (accessed on 8/6/15).

Arricau, Raymond. "Teresa of St. Augustine (Louise of France, 1737-1787)" at http://carmelnet.org/biographies/TeresaStAugustine.pdf (accessed 10/1/15).

Bachelier, Alcime. "*Le Jansénisme à Nantes de 1714 à 1728.*" *Mémoires de la société d'histoire et d'archéologie de Bretagne*, 10 (1929), 55-56.

Baehrel, René. "*Stastitique et démographie historique: la mortalité sous l'ancien régime*," in *Annales. Économies, Sociétés, Civilisations,* 12 (1957), no. 1, 85-98, at http://www.persee.fr/doc/ahess_0395-2649_1957_num_12_1_2603?h=baehrel (accessed 11/6/16).

Barringer, George M. "They Came to Georgetown: The French Sulpicians," *Georgetown Magazine*, July 1977, at http://www.library.georgetown.edu/special-collections/archives/essays/french-sulpicians (accessed Oct. 15, 2015).

Belisaire. "*La population française sous l'Ancien Régime*," at http://www.philisto.fr/cours-75-la-population-francaise-sous-l-ancien-regime.html (accessed 11/2/16).

Brislen, Sr. M. Bernetta. "The Episcopacy of Leonard Neale, Second Archbishop of Baltimore," in *Historical Records and Studies*, XXXIV (New York: The U.S. Catholic Historical Society, 1945), 35.

Campbell, Bernard U. "Desultory Sketches of the Catholic Church in Maryland," II, in *The Religious Cabinet*, Vol. I (Baltimore: John Murphy, 1842), 391-396.

Carroll, Rt. Rev. John. "Letter to Bishop Douglass, March 3, 1791" in *The Catholic Historical Review*, Vol. 5 (Apr. 1919-Jan. 1920), 396-397.

Christol, Arsène. "Dom Augustin de Lestrange (1754-1827)," at http://www.arccis.org/downloads/lestrange.pdf (accessed 11/18/15).

Cuyler, Cornelius. "Pigeon Hill," *The Borromean*, XIII, no. 6 (Nov., 1947), 5-6 and 23.

Dolman, Charles. Review of A. Dick's *Reasons for Embracing the Catholic Faith*, in *Dolmans Magazine and Monthly Miscellany of Criticism*, 1848, 378. GB

Dick, Alexander. "Copy of a letter, dated Edinburg, 28th January, 1804, to the late venerable Mr. Nagot," *The Metropolitan*. Baltimore: T. Blenkinsopp, 1830, 200-204. GB.

[Garnier, Antoine?]. "*Nécrologie*" (Obituary for François-Charles Nagot), in *L'ami de la religion et du roi*, Vol. 8 (Paris: Le Clerc, 1816), 286-288.

Girard, Victor. "*Chateaubriand à vingt-deux ans: d'après des documents inédit*" in *Le Correspondent*, CCXX (1905), 583-594.

Harel, J.-Bruno. "Currateau, John Baptiste" in the *Dictionary of Canadian Biography* at http://www.biographi.ca/en/bio/curatteau_jean_baptiste_4E.html (accessed on 8/4/15).

Lucas, L. "*Deux interessantes thèses de l'histoire locale*," in *L'Ouest-Eclair*, Aug. 25, 1934, 4-5, at http://gallica.bnf.fr/ark:/12148/bpt6k625644t/f4.item (accessed 12/8/15). BNF

McGovern, John. "The Gallipolis Colony in Ohio: 1786-1793," in *Records of the American Catholic Historical Society*, XXXVII (1926), 26-72. GB

Mondésir, Jean-Édouard Piarron de, "Souveniers of Jean Edward de Mondesir," in *The Voice of the Students and Alumni of St. Mary's Seminary*, (Baltimore, MD: St. Mary's Seminary & University) IX, no. 1 (Oct. 1931), 20-25; IX, no. 2 (Nov. 1931), and 22-24; and IX, no. 4 (Jan. 1932), 22-23.

Noguès, Boris. "*La maîtrise ès arts en France aux XVIIe et XVIIIe siècles*," at http://histoire-education.revues.org/2069 (Accessed 1/9/16).

Pound, Pandora, et al. "From Apoplexy to Stroke," in *Age and Ageing*, 26 (1997), 331-337, at http://ageing.oxfordjournals.org/content/26/5/331.full.pdf (accessed on Dec. 8, 2015).

Ryder, H. I. D. "M. Emery, Superior of Saint Sulpice, 1789-1811," *The Dublin Review*, Third Series, 18 (July-Oct. 1887), 243-267.

Salin, Dominique. "La pédagogie jésuite, entre excellence et encouragement," at http://www.jesuites.com/2014/03/la-pedagogie-jesuite-entre-excellence-et-encouragement/ (accessed 10/11/15).

Shane, Scott. "The Secret History of City Slave Trade," at http://articles.baltimoresun.com/1999-06-20/topic/9906220293_1_slave-trade-buy-slaves-slaves-were-sold (accessed 1/11/16).

Watson, William T., M.D. "The Present Decline of Malaria in Maryland," in *Maryland Medical Journal*, XLVIII, no. 8 (August, 1905), 289-302. GB

Anonymous, *Catalogue des Messieurs emploiés dans le Séminaire de Saint Sulpice, et dans ceux qui en dépendent.* Paris: handwritten bound volume in SA., n.d.

Anonymous, *Materiaux pour la vie de Monsieur Emery,* 12 vols. Paris: bound volumes in SA, n.d.

Anonymous. *"Réglement 1769."* Paris: handwritten document in the file entitled, *"Anciens Réglements"* in the SA, 1769.

Anonymous, *Réglement Général du Séminaire de St. Sulpice [à Paris].* Paris: bound calligraphic manuscript in the SA, n.d.

Dubois, Jean, Letter to A. Maréchal, Nov. 23, 1812. Baltimore: handwritten document in the collection of the Associated Sulpicians of the U.S. at the AA.

_____, Letter to J. Carroll, Nov. 28, 1807. Baltimore, Doc. 3 F11 in the collection of the Archdiocese of Baltimore at the AA.

Eaton, Vincent M., ed. and trans. *Necrology of the Society of St. Sulpice, Province of the U.S.* Baltimore: unpublished bound text in the collection of the Associated Sulpicians of the U.S. at the AA, n.d.

Emery, Jacques-André. "Counsels and rules of conduct for the Priests of St. Sulpice sent, in April 1791, to establish a Seminary in Baltimore, in the United States," trans. Anonymous. Baltimore: AA, 1791.

Faillon, Étienne-Michel. *Histoire du séminaire de Saint-Sulpice de Baltimore et les divers établissements aux quels il a donné naissance,* 2 vols. Baltimore, MD: unpublished bound manuscript in the collection of the Associated Sulpicians of the U.S. at the AA, 1861.

Guillerm, Gabrielle. *"La Contribution française aux débuts de l' Église catholique des États-Unis (1790-1850).* Paris: unpublished master's thesis at the Université Paris Sorbonne, 2013, at the SA.

Minutes of the Faculty Meetings of the Baltimore Seminary. trans. R. MacDonough. Baltimore: typed translation in the AA.

Minutes of the General Council, III. Paris: Handwritten bound volume in the SA, Manuscript 23, Vol. III, (1758-1863).

Minutes of the General Assemblies of the Society of Saint Sulpice (*Registre des Assemblées et Congrégations générales*), III. Paris: bound handwritten volume in the SA.

Mouille, J. *Histoire du Grand Séminaire de Nantes.* Paris: typed manuscript in SA, n.d.

Nagot, François-Charles. Nagot Correspondence. Baltimore: Collection of the Associated Sulpicians of the U.S. at the AA.

_____. Nagot Personal Papers, Baltimore: Collection of the Associated Sulpicians of the U.S. at the AA.

Tessier, Jean. *Epoques*. trans. J. J. Kortendick. Baltimore: typed translation in the collection of the Associated Sulpicians of the U.S. at the AA, n.d.

_____. "Historical diary of the Treasurer of the Seminary of Baltimore," trans. J. J. Kortendick. Baltimore: typed translation in the Collection of the Associated Sulpicians of the U.S. at the AA, n.d.

Vaillac, Henri d'Antin de. *Les constitutions de la compagnie de Saint-Sulpice, Étude historique et canonique,* Vol. II. Paris: unpublished doctoral thesis at the Institut Catholique, n.d., in the Collection of the Associated Sulpicians of the U.S. at the SA.